D1263433

The Customer Service Intervention

Bottom-Line Tactics for Front-Line Managers

by
Carolyn A. Martin, Ph.D.
& Bruce Tulgan

HRD PRESS
Amherst, Massachusetts

Copyright © 2003, RainmakerThinking, Inc.

Published by: HRD Press, Inc.
                22 Amherst Road
                Amherst, MA 01002
                800-822-2801 (U.S. and Canada)
                413-253-3488
                413-253-3490 (fax)
                http://www.hrdpress.com

All rights reserved. No part of this book may be
reproduced, stored in a retrieval system, or transmitted
in any form by any means, electronic, mechanical,
photocopying, recording, or otherwise, without the
prior permission of the author.

ISBN: 0-87425-743-3

Cover design by Eileen Klockars
Editorial and production services by Mary George

Printed in Canada

——— CONTENTS ———

—— INTRODUCTION ——

What do we mean by customer service? Our definition is simple: meeting or exceeding the needs and wants of the people buying your services and products. Ultimately, customer service is affected by every process in your business: research, design, production, distribution, marketing, merchandizing, sales, delivery, and so on. While all of these are important, we have chosen to focus on one of the most critical yet overlooked processes of customer service: the day-to-day management of front-line service personnel.

We know that busy supervisory managers, struggling every day to turn front-line people into great service teams, don't have time to read another customer service book. Therefore, we have created a practical, step-by-step program to teach you the essentials:

1. How to quickly assess the effectiveness of your staff
2. How to launch an intervention to keep them service savvy
3. How to seize opportunities every day to improve the quality of every customer interaction

The Customer Service Intervention is that program.

Why do we call it an intervention? Customer service occurs in the context of ongoing business; so focusing acutely on service with the aim of improving it requires stopping in the middle of everything and taking action.

We'll ask you to stop and evaluate your team, yourself, and each team member. We'll urge you to make personnel changes and adjust future hiring criteria. We'll insist that if you want to dramatically improve your team's customer service performance, you must spend substantial amounts of time training your staff in off-site seminars, team meetings, and one-on-one coaching sessions. Any of these steps alone, but surely all of them together, will amount to an intervention.

We also chose the term "intervention" because we want to share with you our sense of urgency about improving customer service and the drastic efforts required to accomplish such improvements.

This program puts the burden squarely on you, the supervisory manager. Why? While an organization can teach the principles and tactics of good customer service to front-liners in many ways, our research indicates that the most effective approach is direct, sustained managerial intervention. You are best qualified to evaluate your team's current state of customer service delivery, to identify bad service syndromes, to take corrective action, and to monitor improvement over time. You also know individual players and are best able to identify problem employees, high-level performers, and potential peer leaders, as well as to control future employee selection. Most important, you are in the best position to build constant customer service training into the routine work environment and to hold employees accountable for implementing that training. So it's all up to you.

Because of our long-running study of young generations in the workplace, many people have asked us if this program is focused on younger service personnel. The answer is yes and no.

We did begin designing the program with the idea of teaching customer service to teenagers, for we saw a pressing need: Young workers are disproportionately represented in front-line customer service positions, and study after study shows that customers complain most about the service provided by younger personnel. However, as we were developing the program, we realized it would be appropriate and effective for front-line service personnel of all ages. We thus widened our focus. The program, then, is intended to inform and empower managers supervising customer service teams with all degrees of age diversity.

Overview of the Pocket Guide

This book presents our Customer Service Intervention program in two main sections:

- **Part 1. The Big Picture.** The six chapters in this section let you know "what to do." They offer a program overview that summarizes the tactics, best practices, and techniques you'll need for your intervention.

- **Part 2. Customer Service Intervention: The Program.** Here "what to do" is translated into "how to do it" through scripts, exercises, activities, tools, and implementation ideas. With this four-stage program, you'll learn how to do all of the following:

  — Prepare for and launch an initial training program in customer service

  — Engage your team in creating customer service information tools

  — Keep your team buzzing about customer service during routine meetings with quick, hard-hitting "quarter-hour courses"

Since support, coaching, and training are the key ingredients to a successful intervention, these easy-to-customize materials will help you introduce and reinforce the basic customer service principles and tactics your front-liners need to master.

If you're like most of the managers we meet, then you know that your team would benefit from a customer service intervention—and you don't need to be convinced about the urgency. Here, then, is what to do and how to do it. Now it's all up to you.

PART I
The Big Picture

CHAPTER I

Assess Your Service

Your service personnel have many opportunities every day to impress, delight, and even dazzle your customers. But if they're going to seize those opportunities, you have to train them, first and foremost, to avoid the pitfalls that make so many front-liners fail. Below are presented 12 of the most common complaints that people have about service personnel. Do any of them apply to your team? Your answer will help you determine the direction your customer service intervention will take.

The 12 Pitfalls: Most Common Customer Complaints About Service People

1. They are nowhere to be found.
2. They are present but unavailable to serve customers.
3. They are available but rude, rushed, or indifferent.
4. They are engaged and polite, but unknowledgeable.
5. They provide customers with misinformation or conflicting information.
6. They are too slow.

7. They make mistakes.

8. They unnecessarily complicate transactions.

9. They are unable to solve small problems.

10. They are unable to deal effectively with customer complaints.

11. They embarrass customers for not doing something correctly.

12. They fail to meet, much less exceed, customer expectations.

The Pitfalls—Underlying Causes

We found that when front-liners consistently receive such complaints, usually one or more of these causes are involved:

1. The front line is overstaffed (leading to lack of urgency) or understaffed (leading to lack of coverage).

2. The team is made up of the wrong people; that is, there are too many low-level, mediocre performers and not enough high-level, outstanding ones.

3. The team lacks the tools and support it needs.

4. Team members don't care about service.

5. Team members have insufficient training in customer service fundamentals.

6. Team members too often lose their focus on service and thus "drop the ball."

7. Team members are not held accountable for delivering dazzling customer service.

● *What Is Your Cash-Register Culture?*

We have developed the term "cash-register culture" to describe the social dynamic that develops among front-line personnel in a customer service workplace. Because front-liners spend so much time together on a regular basis, they build interpersonal relationships. "Customers just pass through," some of them think, "but I spend hours with my coworkers, day after day."

Often these relationships and how they are conducted have a huge impact on the team's ability to deliver customer service. They very easily can distract front-liners from their customers. The key question for you as the supervisory manager is this: Does your cash-register culture focus your front-line personnel on each other—or on your customers?

As mentioned earlier, many business processes have an impact on customer service. However, each of the underlying causes above falls squarely within the realm of your day-to-day supervisory responsibilities: staffing (1, 2), training (3, 5), motivation (4), and performance management (6, 7). These essential processes lie at the heart of any intervention.

Assessing Your Service: Key Steps

We highly recommend that before spending time and energy on staffing, training, motivation, or performance management, you engage with your team in a thorough self-evaluation. You want clear answers to the questions "What's going right with this team and individual?" and "What's going wrong with this team and individual?"

Then you can ask, "What will it take to help this team and individual deliver excellent customer service?"

There are four key steps to this critical requirement:

- **Step 1.** Evaluate your team in terms of the common customer service complaints and their possible underlying causes. Do customers complain about your team in any of the 12 areas we've identified? In any other areas? If so, how often? Why does this happen? What can be done about it?

- **Step 2.** Evaluate your own role in relation to the common complaints and possible underlying causes. Do you contribute to any of these complaints? How? What have you done to address them? Have those steps been effective? What more can you do? Are you willing to make a commitment to eliminating these complaints? Are you willing to commit to playing a more hands-on role as a trainer, coach, and supervisor to make dramatic improvements in your team's delivery of customer service? Are you willing to hold each team member 100 percent accountable for delivering great customer service?

- **Step 3.** Ask members to evaluate their team in terms of the common complaints and possible underlying causes. Does the team consistently receive one or more of these complaints? If so, how often? Why? What do you suggest should be done about it?

- **Step 4.** Ask members to evaluate themselves individually in relation to the common complaints and possible underlying causes. Does the member contribute to one or more of these complaints? How? What has he or she done to improve matters? Have those steps been effective? What more can this member do to improve matters? Is he or she willing to make a commitment to a new customer service mission for this team and be held 100 percent accountable for it? Is the member willing to be a customer service leader on the team?

Part 2 of this pocket guide will provide you with assessment forms for implementing these steps.

CHAPTER 2

Select the Right Players

Without the right people on your team, no customer service intervention will be effective. That's why the critical next step is to conduct a straightforward assessment of each team member. You must assess them in terms of their capacity and inclination to participate in the customer service mission with enthusiasm and diligence. You have to be prepared to remove low-level performers, work on improving mediocre ones, and build your team, step by step, into one filled by only high-level performers.

Assessment Formula: Ability, Skill, Will

How do you assess the performance capacity of individual team members? At RainmakerThinking, we have developed a simple performance-evaluation formula that focuses on three categories:

1. **Ability.** Does the employee have the natural talent and inclination to perform the necessary tasks and responsibilities? If someone lacks the ability to perform, you must either change some of that person's assignments or remove him or her from the team.

2. Skill. Has the employee learned the information and techniques to perform the necessary tasks and meet the necessary responsibilities? If someone lacks the skill to perform, you must either provide additional training or remove the person from the team.

3. Will. Does the employee have the necessary internal motivation and external incentive to perform the required tasks and meet the required responsibilities? If someone lacks the will to perform, you must do one of three things: (1) ask that person to generate the motivation, (2) provide additional incentives, or (3) remove that person from the team.

This formula—ability, skill, will—is immensely useful in evaluating an individual's performance, working with an individual on broad self-evaluation, and developing individual performance improvement plans.

Selecting the Right Players: Key Steps

All together, there are seven important steps to this part of the intervention:

- **Step 1.** Conduct the assessment as explained above, evaluating each team member in terms of his or her ability, skill, and will to perform great customer service. Be honest with yourself. Prepare to be honest with your employees. Identify potential peer leaders, high-level performers, those whose performance needs improvement, and those whom you deem hopelessly low-level performers.

- **Step 2.** Remove hopelessly low-level performers.

- **Step 3.** Focus on team members whose performance needs improvement. Prepare to have a one-on-one meeting with each of them based on the initial, "ability, skill, will" assessment. Focus on concrete opportunities for improvement, set specific performance-improvement goals, and ask each member to commit to improving performance. Be sure to hold follow-up sessions on a regular basis.

- **Step 4.** Based on your initial assessment, your one-on-one meetings, and your follow-up sessions, make a second round of decisions on removing individuals from the team. Once you have made a substantial effort to help them, remove those who are not meeting their specific performance-improvement goals.

- **Step 5.** Review and revise your hiring process and your hiring-selection criteria based on what you've learned from your rigorous assessments of individual team members. Are you testing prospective hires for customer service ability, skill, and will? Are you gearing interviews toward these priorities? Are you gathering concrete proof that the prospect has the personal characteristics and attitude required to interact effectively with customers? Are you making it clear to prospective hires that high performance with respect to customer service is the only option on your team?

- **Step 6.** Prepare to recruit high-level performers to become peer leaders; in this role, they can help you with training and coaching employees in customer service. Begin by reviewing the portions of the service evaluations that refer to leadership and commitment. For now, focus on members whom you identified as high-level performers. Later on, in Stage 2 of the intervention, add to your considerations those who receive nominations from a substantial number of their peers and who indicate a willingness to serve in a leadership capacity.

- **Step 7.** Now you are ready to pull the team together and really get them engaged in, and committed to, your new customer service mission. This step initiates the second stage of the intervention, laid out in greater detail in Part 2. In essence, you will call a series of special team meetings—on- or offsite, depending on your resources, schedule, and preference. In the initial meeting (or first series of meetings), you will introduce your new customer service mission and engage your front-liners in team and individual assessments. You'll begin training on the fundamental principles and skills of customer service, and gear them up for the creative activities and ongoing training that will be part of your ongoing intervention.

In Part 2, you will find a number of tools to help you implement these seven key steps.

CHAPTER 3

Sell Your Team on Customer Service

Managers have asked us, "But how do I get my front-liners to really care about delivering customer service in the first place?" Obviously, it's hard to train people who don't care—and how do you teach caring? Unfortunately, appeals to empathy—"Think of your own experiences as a customer and try to deliver the level of service you prefer"—are not always effective, especially with young workers. Why? Different people have different expectations based on their experiences and tastes. So you can't trust that employee preferences will match customer requirements.

To get your front-liners to really care about delivering great customer service, you have to sell the importance of customer service to them and then keep selling it on an ongoing basis. That means you need a compelling "sales message" that will drive your customer service intervention and convey the principles behind it. You also need to ensure that every member of your team puts the message into action.

In this chapter, we'll take a close look at a model "sales message" and its related action steps.

The Sales Message and Action Steps

To be effective, your message to front-liners should be clear, concise, and workable. Here is precisely the kind of sales message that you want to communicate:

> *"Customer service is non-negotiable. It makes work more enjoyable. It makes everyone's job easier. It is one of the most valuable skills you can possibly master. Every customer is a potential contact worth impressing. So take care of our customers, and we'll take care of you!"*

1. "Customer service is non-negotiable."

To convey this point to your team, you must trumpet the message at every opportunity: "Customer service is what this team is about. Customer service is what we do here. Customer service is the number one reason you are here. That's what we're paying you to do."

Even more important, the message must be absolutely true. This means you must intervene immediately at any instance of poor service. Treat every customer service failure as a crisis, taking time with all the involved employees to debrief them, identify the learning opportunities at hand, and review the steps that should have been taken.

In terms of non-negotiability, you must be prepared to remove team members who repeatedly fail to deliver good customer service. And don't keep it a secret. Make sure the rest of the team knows that the price for poor service is dismissal from your team.

2. "It makes work more enjoyable."

You have to constantly remind team members that good customer service has a huge impact on their ability to enjoy work. When employees are engaged in a task or meeting responsibilities, their behavior is likely to support a positive attitude. A positive attitude increases the enjoyment of any task, but this is especially true when it comes to human interaction. People tend to feed on each other's attitudes, feed back similar signals, and reproduce those attitudes.

Customers who feel ignored, under-served, or rebuffed by front-liners tend to get frustrated and annoyed. They often express those feelings and seek redress, thus creating an uncomfortable atmosphere for employees. In contrast, customers who feel well served tend to reflect their satisfaction, behave in a more relaxed manner, buy more, and express gratitude to service personnel.

3. "It makes everyone's job easier."

You must keep reminding your team that investing effort in good service ultimately saves everyone a lot of time and energy, whereas bad service creates a downward spiral that makes everyone's job harder. Unsatisfied customers are less respectful to employees and to the store; they disrupt store displays, move and spoil merchandise, and buy less; they bad-mouth to other customers and complain to staff.

When this downward spiral takes hold, employees spend a tremendous amount of time and energy soothing bad feelings, solving problems, and cleaning up the mess. If every front-line employee is focused on great service, unnecessary waste is kept to a minimum and employees can use their valuable time and energy to build an upward spiral of success.

4. "It is one of the most valuable skills you can possibly master."

The most ambitious young workers are hungry for training opportunities so they can build skills that will make them more valuable in the job market and in other aspects of their lives. Often they don't realize that customer service, in and of itself, is an extremely valuable skill—one that does not become obsolete. Neither do they often realize that it is a broadly transferable skill— one that makes any employee more valuable in any role in any organization.

With your support, training, and coaching, young employees have an opportunity to become customer service experts. Don't miss a chance to remind them that every single customer service interaction is an opportunity to practice and fine-tune this vital skill. It's a message that will appeal to the more ambitious among them.

5. "Every customer is a potential contact worth impressing."

Also appealing to the more ambitious of young employees will be the idea of networking with customers while delivering great service. You don't want them handing out resumes to impressive-looking customers, of course; but you should remind them that every customer is a potential contact. Regardless of age, size, shape, and attire, every customer has his or her own sphere of influence and authority. Every customer has the potential to help you in one way or another. So what? Your customers are worth impressing. That's what.

How do you impress customers? By doing a fantastic job in your current role. Impressive people are impressed by those who are themselves positive, motivated, polite, and focused on the task at hand. They will notice you. They will remember you. Learn their names, and they might learn yours.

6. "Take care of our customers and we'll take care of you."

Make sure that every team member knows they can earn financial and non-financial rewards by delivering great service to customers. On your part, that means reserving the "desirables"—the best assignments, shifts, and learning opportunities; exposure to decision-makers; days off; cash, gift certificates, and promotional giveaways; and anything else you have to offer—as rewards for customer service excellence.

To ensure this approach is fair, you'll have to be a more hands-on manager, setting goals, monitoring and measuring performance, and holding employees accountable on a daily basis. Reward those who succeed and, just as important, withhold rewards from those who fail. Establish small bonus-style rewards and use them frequently, but be sure to tie every reward directly to specific instances of performance.

CHAPTER 4

Teach the Basics

You may assume that people with technical expertise or college degrees would know how to interact well with customers. Think again. You may assume that everyone should know what it means to be polite, friendly, and professional. Think yet again. The truth is, often front-line service personnel fail to deliver good service simply because they don't know what to do or how to do it.

Your job as manager is to ensure that front-liners develop the human relationship skills needed to serve your customers properly. One effective way to do that is to offer regular and ongoing training—formal or informal, onsite or off. When formal training is unavailable or impractical, you still have at your disposal the day-to-day real lessons—good or bad—that each individual on your team learns in real time with real customers. Such lessons are your informal training curriculum: You recognize successes, reinforce learning, offer reminders of the lessons, and provide coaching. These one-on-one interventions also act as adjuncts to and supports of formal training.

In all cases, then, the bottom line is this: Customer service training is an integral part of your supervisory responsibility—each and every day.

Guidelines for Formal Training

When is formal classroom training necessary and appropriate? When you want to make a big impact on a group or team of employees through a shared experience. Formal training can introduce a new program, provide an overview of information and techniques, and engage participants in interactive exercises and discussions. The length and format should be tailored to fit the teaching-learning agenda at hand.

For delivering customer service training—especially formal training of any length—we offer seven guidelines:

1. Focus on the fundamentals.
2. Keep lessons brief, straight, and simple.
3. Use stories selectively.
4. Use multimedia.
5. Repetition is key.
6. Get trainees involved in the learning.
7. Encourage practice.

I. Focus on the Fundamentals

There is no need to teach front-liners the latest and greatest techniques in communication, marketing, sales, and service. Often such efforts are inappropriate and lead to confusion rather than improved customer service.

Frankly, it is difficult enough to teach basic principles and tactics and get them to stick. We thus recommend that you avoid complicated approaches. Teach people to walk, and if they're so inclined, they'll learn to run on their own.

2. Keep Lessons Brief, Straight, and Simple

The most seasoned trainers will tell you that too much information can complicate a simple lesson. The same goes for lessons that are too clever, too cute, too funny, too elaborate, or too anything. This is especially important to remember if you are not an experienced trainer. Don't make lessons boring, but do choose one point for each lesson and really drive that point home.

3. Use Stories Selectively

A story can be great for illustrating a point, but only if the story is right on point. So don't stretch it. When you can relate a personal experience that truly illustrates the point you're trying to make, then relate it. But keep it short.

4. Use Multimedia

You don't need a laserlight show, but using multimedia will help to drive your points home and make them stick. Focus on just one point in each lesson. Relate the point orally and use various media to reinforce it as often as possible within a short period of time. Also include discussion. For example, you could follow these steps:

1. Present your point orally in conjunction with an overhead slide.
2. Use an audio or video clip; then return to the slide.

3. Use a flip chart and a handout.
4. Facilitate a brief discussion.
5. Make your point orally again.

5. Repetition Is Key

In each lesson, make your point and then repeat it 10 times inside of 10 minutes. You'll have truly made your point, at least for now. Down the road, when you've cycled through every lesson you have to teach, start over again with the first lesson. Make your point, and repeat it as before. And so on.

6. Get Trainees Involved in the Learning

Involve participants, but don't make the mistake of turning over lesson time to them. Control the time and lesson content by asking questions that direct the team as well as involve it. For example:

- "Are you great at this tactic? If so, give us a concrete example of a success story."
- "Do you have room to improve on this tactic?"
- "What will you do today to practice this tactic?"

7. Encourage Practice

End every lesson by clearly assigning trainees to implement the day's lesson with real customers. "Go out there right now and practice this tactic."

Finally, if it is appropriate, turn the lesson into a contest or creative activity with prizes and recognition (see Part 2 of the pocket guide for suggestions).

● *The Fundamental Principle*

If you teach nothing else about customer service, teach this one principle:

"Always under-promise and over-deliver!"

Manage Expectations ...

Ultimately, the secret to delivering great customer service is managing expectations and then exceeding them. Of course, you don't want front-liners to overly lower expectations—that may chase away customers. But they should promise customers a little bit less than whatever they are certain they can deliver. What does that delivery look like in your business? Be sure everyone on your team knows the answer.

Meet Expectations ...

Customers typically come into contact with service personnel because they want to make something happen—gather information, find a service or product, or complete a transaction. What should your front-line service personnel be trying to do? Facilitate making it happen. How? Make it right, make it easy, make it fast.

Exceed Expectations ...

This is the hard part. It means doing everything very well—and then doing more. Service should be better, easier, and faster than the customer could have possibly expected. To provide even more, consider offering free items: samples, which are given before a sale, or add-ons, which are given after a sale. If your industry doesn't usually offer samples, you can set yourself apart by providing them; if samples are industry staples, though, you will have to offer more and better to set yourself apart. Keep in mind that add-ons are just as important, as they reward customers for doing business with you.

Teaching Focus: The Tactical Skills

In teaching, you should focus on two sets of tactical skills:

1. Communication
2. Problem solving

Both communication and problem solving are areas of great complexity and nuance. Here we will keep it simple by recommending that, in teaching, you focus on their basics as related to the customer service environment.

Communication

Your trainees should learn and thoroughly understand these eight communication keys:

1. Make yourself available.
2. Listen carefully.
3. Say as little as possible.
4. Rely on prepared materials whenever possible.
5. Be truthful.
6. Request feedback.
7. Always say ...
8. Never say ...

1. Make Yourself Available

Being available doesn't necessarily require approaching customers, making eye contact, smiling, and extending greetings, although this is the method favored by some organizations. In our view, such details are a matter of style. What is essential is that front-liners respond to customers as needed. What does that require? Being both physically and mentally present—being visible to customers and paying close attention to their words and actions.

2. Listen Carefully

Listening is the most important and least practiced communication skill. How does someone practice it? Through any and every conversation, in the following way:

- *First,* use both eyes and ears.
- *Second,* do not interrupt when someone else is speaking.
- *Third,* don't let your mind wander: Concentrate.
- *Fourth,* ask open-ended questions such as "Can you tell me more about that?" and "Can you give me an example?"
- *Fifth,* when you think you understand what the other person is saying, ask specific, clarifying questions such as "Do you mean [possible meaning]?" or "Do I understand correctly that you are saying [what person may be saying]?"

3. Say as Little as Possible

The rationale behind this fundamental may be expressed as follows: The less you say,

—the less chance there is of saying something distracting, confusing, annoying, wrong, or offensive;

—the less time is consumed by your words;

—the more air space customers will have to talk (and most people prefer talking to listening);

—the more likely you will be to choose your words
very carefully.

Saying as little as possible, however, does not mean
saying nothing. It means that service personnel must
listen carefully to customers, stop and think, choose
the right words, and respond succinctly.

4. Rely on Prepared Materials Whenever Possible

The beauty of prepared materials is that they tend to
reflect a substantial amount of research, judgment, planning, content selection, design, and production. Thus,
they almost always provide a more thorough, precise,
and attractive response than most front-liners are capable
of offering. Thus it is important to do the following:

1. Make available to front-line personnel good prepared materials on services, products, processes,
   and issues about which customers often inquire.

2. Ensure that front-liners are sufficiently familiar
   with such materials to make good use of them.
   This means knowing what materials are available,
   what they say, and where to find them.

Chapter 5 describes a variety of information tools that
would benefit your team; also, Stage 3 of our program
shows you how to involve your team in their development
through a series of workshops.

5. Be Truthful

While this may seem like a no-brainer, it is more important in practice than some people might realize. Of

course, service personnel should not lie to customers. But being truthful goes far beyond the obvious "don't lie" rule. It targets the small inaccuracies that inadvertently irritate and damage trust. Such inaccuracies usually result from hopes, guesses, and exaggerations. What is the solution?

- *First,* don't express hopes out loud to customers.
- *Second,* don't make guesses out loud to customers.
- *Third,* don't exaggerate out loud to customers. If something is going to take 10 minutes, don't say it will take "a couple of minutes"; instead say, "at least 10 minutes."

What if front-liners don't know the answer to a customer inquiry? The flat-out rule is, don't guess. They should say, "I don't know. Let me find out for you." If it's appropriate to the situation, they should add, "Let me collect your contact information so I can get the correct answer to you."

6. Request Feedback

If your organization has a formal system for collecting customer feedback, encourage customers to use it. But the most useful feedback is not what goes into a central clearinghouse of information to be sorted through and interpreted by corporate analysts. The feedback that you need as a supervisory manager is feedback about things you can control—inventory; display; atmosphere; your team's overall quality, ease, and speed; and anything noteworthy about individuals on your team.

What feedback do front-liners need to request from every customer after every interaction? They simply need to confirm that the customer is happy and has no unsatisfied expectation or need at the moment. That can be accomplished by asking, "Is that acceptable?" Or "Are you happy with everything?" Or "Is there anything else you need?"

7. Always Say ...

Many organizations provide front-liners with company-tailored scripts for various types of customer interactions. Whatever scripts your organization may use, make sure that front-liners have a chance to rehearse so they are prepared to use them with confidence.

We strongly recommend also teaching some basic rules of polite interaction. For example, as appropriate, front-liners should say, "Please," "Thank you," and "You're welcome." When greeting a customer, they should ask, "How may I help you?" Following an interaction, they should ask, "Are you happy with everything?" or "Is there anything else you need?"

8. Never Say ...

Again, this is often a matter of style and each organization is different in its preferences. Still, we feel confident in saying that front-liners should never curse; never comment about a customer, coworker, or vendor; never speak in a raised voice or with a disrespectful tone; and never say, "I can't help you."

Problem Solving

These are the six keys of successful problem-solving in a customer service context:

1. Be on the lookout for problems great and small.

2. Distinguish problems you can solve from problems you can't solve.

3. Solve small problems here and now if possible.

4. Give special treatment to bigger problems.

5. Engage complaining customers.

6. Take ownership of customer complaints.

I. Be on the Lookout for Problems Great and Small

Before you can begin to solve problems, you must become adept at identifying them. So what exactly is a problem? Simply put, it's something begging for a solution. In the context of customer service, problems usually come in one of two types:

- *The customer complaint.* This is not always easy to handle but is usually easy to identify.

- *The missing, out of place, or broken "something."* Identifying this type of problem usually requires being on the lookout for hassle-making situations that slow or confuse a transaction or that irritate and frustrate customers. This type of problem also frustrates front-liners because they appear unknowledgeable or inept. In many cases, such problems are "fires" that must be put out immediately because they distract everyone from their service focus.

2. Distinguish Problems You Can Solve From Problems You Can't Solve

"You" means front-liners, who are not always the right people to solve the problems they identify. When they do identify a problem, they need to ask, "Do I have the expertise and authority to solve this right here and now, or do I need to find someone who does?"

Obviously, the more experience, training, and coaching that front-liners have, the better equipped they'll be to handle difficult situations as those arise.

3. Solve Small Problems Here and Now If Possible

One of the most rewarding experiences for employees and customers is having problems solved immediately. If the problem is one of those recurring fires, employees should make a note of the date, time, problem, and solution, and sign the note and bring it to your attention. Of course, be prepared to recognize and reward people who contribute once-and-for-all solutions.

4. Give Special Treatment to Bigger Problems

With bigger problems—ones that require greater ability and higher authority to solve—front-line personnel should gather information and pass it to the right person as soon as possible. The key is gathering as much information as possible—the date, time, and details, including the names and contact information of anyone involved.

Front-liners should then immediately get that information into the hands of a manager or someone else who can solve the problem.

Once the problem has been passed on, front-liners are obliged to follow up until they receive confirmation that the problem has been solved. In addition to ensuring the customer's needs have been met, this follow-up is a learning opportunity. How was the situation handled? What procedures were used? What information was needed to resolve it? Is that information readily available for future reference? Does the front-liner now have the know-how to handle similar situations in the future?

5. Engage Complaining Customers

Whether a customer is complaining directly or indirectly, front-line employees must be prepared to engage complaining customers. How? By following the communication tactics we have outlined:

- Make yourself available. In the case of a complaint, ask, "Is something wrong? What can I do to help you?"

- Listen carefully. Be attentive and never interrupt. Ask open-ended questions. With complaints it is important to ask specific, clarifying questions.

- Say as little as possible. Stop and think, choose the right words, and respond succinctly.

- Rely on prepared materials whenever possible.

- Be truthful. Don't lie, don't express hopes, don't exaggerate, and don't make guesses.

- Request feedback. Once you have a plan to solve the customer's problem or pass the complaint to someone who can, ask permission to share your plan and then ask permission to proceed with it. Ask if the customer is satisfied with your plan.

- In the case of customer complaints, always say, "I am sorry" and "Thank you for bringing this to my attention."

- In the case of customer complaints, never argue and never say, "I can't help you."

6. Take Ownership of Customer Complaints

As soon as a front-liner becomes aware of a customer complaint, that complaint becomes the front-liner's problem until the complaint is resolved. This means that when it comes to customer complaints, employees should follow the first through fourth problem-solving fundamentals:

- Be on the lookout. Remember, customers don't always come out and complain. Sometimes they just look disgruntled or mutter unhappily.

- Distinguish solvable problems from the unsolvable. Be aware, however, that you own the problem whether or not you can solve it. Become the customer's liaison and consultant for purposes of resolution.

- Solve small problems here and now if possible. Dazzle customers by addressing and resolving the problem faster and easier than they could possible expect.

- With bigger problems, gather information and pass it to the appropriate person as soon as possible.

Whether the problem is small or big, solved right away or passed on to someone else, when it comes to customer complaints, front-liners should always gather the following information: date, time, nature of the problem, and customer name and contact information. And they should always follow up until they receive confirmation that the problem has been solved: It is the employee's problem until it is solved.

Finally, it is vital that front-liners ask themselves: *What have I learned from the situation that would help me handle a similar problem in the future? Do I now have the expertise and authority to do that?*

Create Just-in-Time Information Tools

It's common sense: Front-line service personnel who are knowledgeable about your organization and its processes, services, and products are better able to serve your customers. As part of your service training, then, we recommend you build up your employees' knowledge through the development of just-in-time information tools. These tools may be high tech (a searchable database) or low tech (a filing cabinet), comprehensive (a book on every issue) or basic (one-page tip sheets). What matters most is that they're easy to use and readily available and that front-liners get in the habit of using them.

Before taking action to develop information tools, see if your organization already has similar materials in place. They may be sufficient for your purposes. Whether such tools are available or you have to build them may determine how comprehensive and technological they will be.

Developing the Tools

If you have to build the information tools yourself, get your team involved in the process. This will not only make it easier on you as the manager, but increase the quality of the tools, provide your team members with a fantastic learning experience, and give team members a feeling of ownership. In Part 2 of this book, we have dedicated an entire stage of the customer service intervention to working with your team to build these information tools.

Once you've completed the development work, the tools will serve as day-to-day job aids for every employee as well as vehicles for ongoing learning. They also will become invaluable for accelerating the initial training of new employees. Be sure to provide copies to the appropriate leaders in your organization so they can make the tools available to other teams. Keep in mind that you, as the supervisory manager, have the responsibility to review, finalize, and distribute any and all information tools.

Six Just-in-Time Information Tools

The following six tools will provide significant support to front-line personnel in delivering service to your customers:

1. Answers to frequently asked questions (FAQs)

2. One-page customer handouts

3. Basic service and product facts

4. Written standard operating procedures (SOPs)

5. "Go-to" people list

6. Complaint process guidelines and forms

I. Answers to Frequently Asked Questions

By its nature, this may be the most useful of all information tools. Here is the best way to develop it:

1. Ask employees to pay close attention over the course of a week to the questions customers most frequently ask. Have them submit those questions to you.

2. Use the submissions as a basis for a training session. In the session, teach front-liners how to write short, concise answers to the questions, and have them practice delivering the answers—it's one thing to write answers and another to deliver them orally with ease and confidence.

3. Finally, create a process for the ongoing documentation of FAQs. Most information tools require continuous development. You may not know you need additions or corrections until situations arise that demand them.

By initially investing time in training front-liners on this tool (and, as we suggest in Part 2, on all information tools that you develop), they become active participants in customer service improvement. Not only will they be a valuable resource to you, but they will be learning valuable skills in the process.

2. One-Page Customer Handouts

After FAQs, this is the next most important resource to create. Sometimes a handout is the best answer a front-liner can provide to a customer. Among the many virtues of handouts is that you can ensure they will be graphically appealing, thorough, and accurate, with all the *i's* dotted and *t's* crossed.

Consider preparing one-pagers for every service, product, process, or issue that inspires a lot of customer questions. Get team members involved in creating them. Assign one to each member—or pair of members—and let them create drafts that you finalize.

3. Basic Service and Product Facts

If your service and product inventory is too broad to provide a comprehensive resource, focus on two categories of services and products:

- Your leading services and products
- The services and products that routinely generate customer questions

Suppliers often provide brochures that contain most of the information your front-liners need. However, ensure that the most important information about any service or product is clear and available to them: What is the service? How do customers access it? Where is the product? How do customers get their hands on it and buy it?

4. Written Standard Operating Procedures (SOPs)

SOPs should be prepared for every task and responsibility that front-liners may be expected to perform. No task or responsibility is too small to warrant SOPs. That doesn't mean SOPs have to be long or complex, though. Often they can be as simple as a few bullet points.

Here is the best way to develop this tool:

1. Brainstorm a list of all the tasks that front-liners must perform and all the responsibilities that they must meet. The list must be comprehensive.

2. Split up the list among team members and ask them to draft bullet-point SOPs for several tasks. Make sure to assign members tasks with which they have direct experience.

3. Circulate the drafts and ask team members to improve on the SOPs for each task.

Again, as the manager, you have the responsibility to review the SOPs and finalize them.

5. "Go-To" People List

This is simply a list of the names of key people and their contact information. Key people include other employees, managers, product/service suppliers, consultants, and service providers. They should correspond to every issue—problem or opportunity—that could possibly arise. Ideally, for every potential issue, you should include a minimum of two "go-to" people. If something comes up that a front-liner cannot personally deal with, he or she should always know whom to contact for help.

6. Complaint Process Guidelines and Forms

There are two key components to the complaint process information tool:

1. Guidelines for handling small matters, that is, matters which lie within the discretion of front-line personnel. These guidelines should define the parameters of that discretion (for example, a dollar limit, flexible policies) as well as the steps to follow when exercising it.

2. A written form for documenting customer complaints that are beyond the front-liner's discretion. This form should provide space to record the date, time, customer's name, contact information, specific complaint, and requested solution.

Ensure that front-liners know they must immediately give the filled-out complaint form to a person with sufficient authority to solve the problem—this is most important.

Finally, as mentioned earlier in our discussion of problem solving, front-line employees must be prepared to follow up with the complaining customer.

Developing each of these just-in-time information tools requires an investment of time and energy. However, the return on that investment can be tremendous. As the supervisory manager, you'll have to lead the charge. In Part 2 of this pocket guide, you'll learn how to charge up your team members by involving them in this development process.

CHAPTER 6

Train, Coach, Reward and **Remind**

Even if they care, even if they know what to do and how to do it, sometimes front-line service personnel lose focus or simply forget to deliver good customer service. That's why you have to remind them of their obligations, and reinforce learning, at every opportunity every day. When it comes to customer service, you simply cannot remind employees too often or too enthusiastically. This is a case where more is always better; so build brief reminders into every part of the workday.

The Ongoing Reminders

Keep your team focused on good customer service by basing your strategy on the following:

1. Team meetings
2. Manager as coach
3. Golden opportunities
4. The individual logbook
5. Peer leaders
6. Customer commendations

7. Signage
8. Games and rewards

I. Team Meetings

If you don't hold regular team meetings, start doing so. Even if you meet only once a week, every meeting should include customer service reminders. Try building a brief customer service lesson into each meeting. Part 2 offers a series of "quarter-hour courses" to help you do this.

2. Manager as Coach

In an ideal world, every manager would meet daily with every single direct report to discuss two key issues:

- "What do you need from me?"
- "Here's what I need from you."

Every day, managers should coach employees on concrete goals and deadlines, spell out guidelines, identify potential problems and resource needs, and provide feedback and suggestions for improvement.

If you are not meeting one-on-one with every direct report for at least 10 minutes at least twice a week, you should start. And when you do, you should devote at least 5 minutes of one of those meetings to remind each person of the customer service focal point of the week.

3. Golden Opportunities

Everytime you observe an employee interacting with a customer, you have a golden opportunity to remind that employee (and any nearby) of customer service principles and tactics. If you see an interaction that could be improved, stop and take the time to privately coach the employee in question:

- Explain what you observed.
- Detail what the employee did right, should have done differently, and could improve the next time. Be specific; for example, "The next time you interact with a customer, I want you to do [this exact thing]."

An equally important opportunity presents itself when you see an employee delivering great customer service. Always take time to stop and commend the employee:

- Explain what you observed.
- Detail what the employee did right. Say "Thank you" and let the employee know how much you appreciate what you observed. Again, be specific; for example, "The next time you interact with a customer, I want you to do [exactly the same thing]!"

4. The Individual Logbook

Ask front-liners to keep a logbook on their customer service. A plain notebook will do. Employees keep track of their service by logging their experiences in three areas:

- How did I dazzle a customer today?
- What was my biggest customer service challenge today?
- What was my biggest customer service mistake today, and what did I learn from it?

This strategy will be much more effective if you provide opportunities for employees to share their logbook entries with you, fellow team members, and others in the organization. It is also critical to provide employees with financial and non-financial rewards for their contributions.

5. Peer Leaders

Select peer leaders by identifying high-level performers who are willing to take on this responsibility and who are nominated by their peers.

What role should they play? That depends upon the supervisory manager. But remember: You're offering ad hoc leadership opportunities to rising stars who can be quite valuable if managed properly. In themselves, they become further reminders of the customer service focus.

Here are some helpful guidelines to follow:

- Carefully select the leaders, using the criteria mentioned above.
- Provide support and training.
- Give them resources and time to learn, grow, and become innovative in their roles.
- Coach them and reward them for succeeding in their roles.

Encourage peer leaders to meet as a group to develop their own ideas, strategies, and initiatives. They should coach their peers in customer service, take turns in team meetings leading discussions and training modules, and lead customer service initiatives.

6. Customer Commendations

Provide customers with information about the following:

- Your customer service initiatives as they are launched
- The standards you are asking service personnel to meet

Then give customers a wealth of easy opportunities to provide input on customer service, especially commendations for high-quality service. The latter are your success stories and act as positive reinforcements and reminders for front-liners.

Deal with commendations in this way:

- Create forms requesting the date, time, and details of the success story, including the name of the service employee involved.
- Encourage customers to share their stories by making the process as easy as possible. You might also offer incentives such as free samples and add-ons, or enter all commending customers into a contest.

7. Signage

Printed reminders of customer service principles and tactics can be very effective. What would they say? Things like this:

- "Always under-promise and over-deliver!"
- "Take care of our customers, and we'll take care of you!"

- "Listen carefully!"
- "Be on the lookout for problems!"

How do you make those printed reminders visible? By putting them on posters, mugs, buttons, tattoos, hats, shirts, pens—anything on which you can print a slogan. How do you make those reminders especially effective? Get the team involved in creating the slogans and choosing the specialty items on which the slogans will appear. Make it a contest. Provide a budget and let the team decide what reminders to create.

8. Games and Rewards

While customer service is a serious business, it doesn't have to be presented seriously. Throughout your training and coaching, become as innovative as you can with fun activities, customer service games, and every possible opportunity for recognizing and rewarding those who significantly and consistently contribute to the mission.

Ask your team what "lights their fire" in terms of rewards. You'll find the answers as varied as the members themselves. They may want gift certificates to restaurants or music stores; bigger discounts from your own business; one-time cash bonuses; time off; or entry into a drawing for larger prizes such as TVs or DVD players. Create a menu of rewards and use those rewards to drive performance. Let front-liners know they'll have ample opportunity to "learn and earn" as they contribute to your customer service mission.

PART 2

Customer Service Intervention:
The Program

—PROGRAM OVERVIEW—

Now that you know what a customer service intervention demands, it's time to implement it. The four stages of our program prepare you to launch your initial training program and engage your front-liners in ongoing customer service initiatives. Stages 1 and 2 logically follow one another, but feel free to prioritize the training modules in stages 3 and 4 to meet your needs.

Stage 1: Prepare for Liftoff

As mentioned earlier, before you take any action, you need to perform a thorough evaluation of you, your team, and each service staffer. The information you discover about staffing, training, motivation, and performance will help determine the priorities for your intervention.

Stage 2: Launch the Program

This train-the-trainer section teaches you how to present your initial training program in a step-by-step format. It contains suggested topics, scripts, time frames, exercises, and activities for full-day, half-day, and two-hour sessions. You will learn how to sell the idea of customer service to your team, engage them in team- and self-evaluations, and begin training them on basic service principles and skills.

Stage 3: Develop Just-in-Time Information Tools

Here you'll learn how to facilitate a series of ongoing workshops to engage your team in creating the information tools needed to deliver more effective service.

Stage 4: Commit to Ongoing Service Training

This section teaches you how to create a series of quarter-hour courses that will keep your team buzzing about customer service. Whether you're reviewing the basics or teaching new skills, you'll find these training modules highly useful. You can easily build them into your weekly team meetings, teach your peer leaders to present them, and follow up with contests, prizes, and recognition for great performers. They are powerful tools in your commitment to ongoing service training.

Prepare for Liftoff

This section will help you identify the challenges and problems that you and your team presently face with customer service. There are two main parts:

1. Assessing your service
2. Selecting the right players

I. Assessing Your Service

Find some quiet time to complete the evaluation tools on the next pages. Be brutally honest. Anything less will dilute the power of your intervention. Record your responses in a notebook or computer file so that you can easily examine major areas of concern.

After you have completed these tools, summarize your conclusions about the effectiveness of your service team as well as about your own management practices.

- What patterns emerge?
- What priorities for intervention are now apparent?

The answers to these questions will help you focus your customer service training program.

Assessment 1A
Evaluating Your Service

PART ONE: Customer Complaints

Directions: Listed below are 12 of the most common customer complaints about service people. Do customers ever make any of these complaints about your team? Circle your response. After each "Yes" response, ask yourself:

- *How often does this happen?*
- *Why does this happen?*
- *Which team members are involved?*
- *What can we do about this?*

Be sure to list any other customer complaints about your team.

Complaints About Service People	Yes/No
1. They are nowhere to be found.	Y / N
2. They are present but unavailable to serve customers.	Y / N
3. They are available but rude, rushed, or indifferent.	Y / N
4. They are engaged and polite, but unknowledgeable.	Y / N
5. They provide customers with misinformation or conflicting information.	Y / N
6. They are too slow.	Y / N
7. They make mistakes.	Y / N
8. They unnecessarily complicate transactions.	Y / N
9. They are unable to solve small problems.	Y / N
10. They are unable to deal effectively with customer complaints.	Y / N
11. They embarrass customers for not doing something correctly.	Y / N
12. They fail to meet, much less exceed, customer expectations.	Y / N

➡

Other complaints customers have about my team:

PART TWO: Your Contributions

Directions: Answer the following questions as honestly as possible.

1. Do you contribute to any of the customer complaints that you have noted? If so ...

   • *Which ones?*

   • *How do you contribute?*

   • *What have you done to address them?*

   • *Have those steps been effective?*

   • *What more can you do?*

2. Are you willing to make a commitment to eliminating these complaints?

Assessment 1B
Customer Complaints: The Causes

Directions: The following questions will help you assess your team on the seven underlying causes of customer complaints. Circle your yes/no responses and answer further questions as needed.

Ask Yourself ...   **Yes/No**

1. Is my team overstaffed (leading to a lack of urgency)? Y / N
   Is it understaffed (leading to a lack of coverage)?   Y / N

   • What is causing these staffing problems?

2. Is my team made up of the wrong people?   Y / N

   • Who are the low-level performers?

   • Who are the mediocre performers?

   • Who are the high-level performers?

   • Who are potential peer leaders?

3. Does my team lack the tools and support it needs?   Y / N

   • What tools would help the team become more
     effective at delivering excellent service?

➡

- What kind of support do I offer the team? How can I do this better?

___

4. Do team members care about service? Y / N

   - Have I made customer service the focus of their daily activities?

   - How do I reinforce the fact that their primary job is to serve customers?

   - How can I do a better job engaging the team in caring about our customers?

___

5. Do team members have sufficient training in customer service fundamentals? Y / N

   - What kind of customer service training have I offered them?

   - Where are the gaps between the team's current skills and knowledge and what they need in order to do an excellent job?

   - Do I provide them with ongoing training in the fundamentals?

➡

Assessment 1B concluded

6. Do team members too often lose their focus on
   service and thus "drop the ball"?   Y / N

   • If so, why does this happen?

   • What is happening in the business or on the team
     that makes members lose focus?

   • How can I refocus them?

7. Are team members held accountable for delivering
   dazzling customer service?   Y / N

   • How do I send the message every day that every
     person has the accountability for delivering dazzling
     customer service?

   • What methods can I use to reinforce this message?

   • Am I willing to commit to playing a more hands-on
     role as a trainer, coach, and supervisor to make
     dramatic improvements in my team's delivery of
     customer service? If so, how will I do this?

Please note that employees can also use these assessment tools; however, we recommend their using the tools that are tailored for employee and team self-evaluations, built into Stage 2 of the program.

2. Selecting the Right Players

Now look more closely at each individual player—you want to get the right team on board. Refer to the information provided earlier in Chapter 2, and be sure to do the following:

1. For your close-up assessment, use the ability, skill, will formula. Identify low-level, mediocre, and high-level performers, and look for potential peer leaders.

2. Review your list of performers and consider what initial actions you will take with each person. Here are some guidelines:

   • *Hopelessly low-level performers.* If you have enough supportive documentation, you may simply want to let these go—make sure you've dotted your *i's* and crossed your *t's* beforehand. Or you may prefer to have one final conversation with them that conveys "Improve or you're out of here." If they commit to improving immediately, you commit to the day-by-day coaching and monitoring of their performance. The first time they backslide, you remove them from the team.

   • *Mediocre performers.* Immediately create a performance improvement plan to get these on track.

- *High-level performers.* "Red flag" those who have the ability to become peer leaders. Prepare to engage them in ongoing training to help you implement your customer service program.

3. Plan to meet one-on-one with your low-level and mediocre performers to discuss their performance. To prepare for the meetings, review your "ability, skill, will" assessments and draft a performance improvement analysis for each person—this will serve as the basis for the meeting. Using the analysis form that we have provided, be sure to do the following:

- Identify the tasks and responsibilities that need review.

- Analyze the source of the problem.

- Record your recommendations for improvement.

Be honest with yourself and prepare to be honest with your employees.

At each meeting, explain the ability, skill, will framework and get the employee's input; then focus the discussion on concrete opportunities to improve performance. Detail a performance improvement plan using the form we have provided. Treating the plan as a contract, ask the employee to commit to improving performance and set specific goals and deadlines. Be prepared to follow up on a regular basis. If someone is not willing to improve, immediately remove him or her from the team.

● *Performance Improvement Analysis*

Employee's Name: **Date:**

Tasks/Responsibilities under review	Ability (Change)	Skill (Training)	Will (Incentives)
1.			
2.			
3.			
4.			
5.			

Recommendations:

● *Performance Improvement Plan*

Employee's Name: **Date:**

Tasks/Responsibilities/ Goals	Actions	Deadline
1.		
2.		
3.		
4.		
5.		

Signatures:

_____   _____
     (Manager)   (Employee)

4. Once you have made a substantial effort to help employees, decide whether you need to remove any from the team. Base this round of decisions on your initial assessments, your one-on-one meetings, and your follow-up sessions. Anyone who is not meeting his or her specific performance improvement goals should be removed.

5. Eventually—but sooner rather than later—you will want to review and revise your hiring process and hiring-selection criteria based on what you've learned from the rigorous assessment of your team. As a starting point, ask yourself:

- Am I testing prospective hires for customer service ability, skill, and will?

- Am I gearing interviews toward these priorities?

- Am I gathering concrete proof that the prospect has the personal characteristics and attitude required to interact effectively with customers?

- Am I making it clear to prospective hires that high performance in customer service is the only option on my team?

6. Prepare to recruit peer leaders. As mentioned in Chapter 2, review your service evaluations and focus on members whom you identified as high-level performers. In Stage 2, add to your considerations those who receive nominations from a substantial number of their peers and who indicate a willingness to serve in a leadership capacity.

Launch the Program

Once you have completed the Stage 1 evaluations and conducted your one-on-one meetings, your intervention has begun. You are now ready to work on launching your new customer service mission and first training program.

Logistics and Preparation

The Logistics

Take an upfront approach to deciding the basics:

- When to launch your program—date and time
- Where to hold the program—onsite or off-site
- How much time to dedicate to the first meeting—a full day, two half-days, or several two-hour sessions
- How to announce the launch—through a memo, meeting, email, and/or voice mail

Prepare Your Materials and Rehearse Them

Here are some helpful guidelines:

- Carefully study all Stage 2 materials. Decide which topics, exercises, and activities to use in your program—not all may be pertinent to your team right now.

- Modify the materials as needed:

  — Adapt our "sales message" in Chapter 3 to make it compelling to your team.

  — Add any additional customer complaints and underlying causes that you discovered through the service evaluations.

  — Customize each Stage 2 worksheet to fit your situation.

- Create an interactive customer service workbook that you can use for training now and for review and reference later on. Consider putting it in a binder or online so that you can add materials developed after the program. If possible, get away from boring black and white and create colorful, user-friendly handouts filled with eye-catching graphics, cartoons, and photos. Think *USA Today,* not employee manual.

- Decide how to position each topic and rehearse your presentation. If you're a seasoned trainer, you already know the importance of practicing what you're going to say and how you're going to say it. Use your own style, humor, stories, insights, examples, experience, and pacing. Be as ingenious and flexible as you wish.

Remember: The key to a successful program lies in preparation, practice, and customization.

Program Outline

Here is an outline of our suggested topics and time frames for a full-day program. Don't forget to schedule time for breaks.

— PROGRAM OUTLINE —

Section A: Introduction and Evaluation

1.	Introduce program and agenda	20–25 min.
2.	Facilitate team evaluations	30–40 min.
3.	Solicit feedback, set priorities, create action plans	50–60 min.
4.	Facilitate individual evaluations	10–15 min.

Section B: Strategies and Training

5.	Teach strategies for "Always under-promise and over-deliver"	45–60 min.
6.	Facilitate training in communication skills	45–60 min.
7.	Facilitate training in problem-solving skills	75–90 min.

Section C: Team Project and Wrap-Up

8.	Engage team in creating "reminders"	35–45 min.
9.	Wrap up program	15–20 min.

For two half-day programs, cover topics 1 through 5 the first day and 6 through 9 the second day. For several 1- to 2-hour sessions, divide topics in a way that makes sense to you.

The following leader's guide covers each section of the program and includes leader's notes and suggested scripting. To make the guide more user-friendly, the participant materials are presented in a group at the guide's conclusion. There are six items:

Section A: Introduction and Evaluation

- Team Evaluation: Customer Service
- Priorities for Implementation
- Self-Evaluation: Customer Service

Section B: Strategies and Training

- The Eight Keys to Successful Communication
- The Six Keys to Successful Problem-Solving
- From Learning Points to Reminders

Leader's Guide

Section A: Introduction and Evaluation

1. Introduce Program and Agenda   20–25 min.

LEADER'S NOTE: Throughout your introduction, set the tone of urgency for the training program. Refer to your organization's mission and commitment to customer service. If your department has its own customer service mission, use it. Have copies available for reference or print it on the first page of your handouts. Briefly review the values and behaviors that your organization teaches about customer service; then make the points presented in the following leader's script.

SCRIPT: It's one thing for our business to stress the importance of customer service; it's another for this team—and everyone on it—to excel at customer service. Since customers are the reason why we're in business in the first place, and why we get a paycheck in the second, we all need to become better every day at meeting and exceeding customer needs. Today is the start of an enthusiastic commitment on my part and—I'm counting on it—on your part as well to learning how to improve customer service.

It's no secret that I've already begun meeting with team members to create performance improvement plans in the area of customer service. [*Optional statement if true:* And it's no secret that we've lost some people because they could not—or would not—make the commitment to improve performance.]

Everyone here today has shown the ability, skill, and will needed to become engaged in and committed to delivering great customer service. However, if at any time during today's program you realize you'd rather not, or can't, make the improvements we'll demand of each other, let me know. I need a 100 percent commitment from every one of you. Participation and commitment are conditions for continued employment.

It's OK if you don't want to, or can't, meet these conditions. That simply means you choose not to remain on this team and we can part as friends. However, let me assure those of you who are ready to participate and commit that I will provide you with tools, support, training, and coaching at every step of the way, day by day. That's my commitment to you so we can all succeed in delivering expert service. Any questions so far? [*Entertain questions.*]

Now I'd like to share some insights into our customer service mission that will drive everything we do and learn today—and beyond today. Please take a look at our "sales message." [*Direct members to location in participant materials and/or refer them to flip chart.*]

LEADER'S NOTE: Read aloud your entire "sales message"; then go back through it, explaining each idea in a way that conveys your passion and commitment. You want the team to realize this is not just another training day, not just another "fad." Remember: The message contains the driving principles supporting your customer service mission. When you say, "Customer service is non-negotiable," the team should know you really mean it.

Now engage members in a discussion, answering their questions and handling any concerns. Tell them that at the program's end, you'll help them create ways to keep the customer service principles at the forefront of everyone's mind. At the end of the discussion, return to the script and present today's agenda.

SCRIPT: On today's agenda, we have a three-part program. The first part focuses on assessments and commitments. I've spent a lot of time thinking about and observing what we do well as a team and as individuals, and what we don't do so well. Now it will be your turn. We'll spend a significant amount of time evaluating the team and ourselves as individuals. Then we'll engage in creating action plans for improvement, setting deadlines, and assigning accountabilities. Again, I'm looking for 100 percent participation and commitment from each of you.

Part two of our program is a crash course on the fundamental principles and skills of customer service. Some of you already know these, and some of you actually use them, but all of us can improve in these areas. Over the next few weeks, we'll be focusing carefully on what we learn today to make sure this training "takes." It's one thing to learn something; it's quite another to translate that learning into action. And I'm definitely looking for action.

Finally, in the third part of our program, we'll start a fun project that will keep what we learn and discuss today in view everywhere we look. But more about that later.

LEADER'S NOTE: Set time frames for the day, including breaks, lunch, and wrap-up time. If you've chosen the half-day or two-hour formats, adjust the time frames accordingly.

2. Facilitate Team Evaluations   30–40 min.

SCRIPT: The first thing we need to do is take stock of what we're doing well and where we need to improve as a team. So, before I make the assignment, I'd like to divide you into smaller teams.

LEADER'S NOTE: If you have five or fewer participants, divide them into two groups or have them work as one. With six or more, definitely divide them into groups with a minimum of three and a maximum of six members.

SCRIPT: Now I need each team to select a facilitator, a timekeeper, and a note-taker. The facilitator will keep you all on track and ensure everyone has a chance to contribute to the discussion. The timekeeper will keep an eye on the clock. The note-taker will take notes and report the team's findings to the room at large; the note-taker will also submit any pertinent results to me after the program. Please volunteer for—or delegate—these tasks right now. [*Allow teams a minute to make selections.*]

LEADER'S NOTE: If possible, provide note-takers with desk- or laptops and projection equipment; if not, flip charts and/or handouts will work fine. Either way, ask note-takers to send you the results electronically after the program. Keep in mind that you, as manager, are responsible for revising, finalizing, and distributing all customer service materials; thus, creating a stream-lined process from the outset will save you time and energy in the long run.

Now ask members to turn to the worksheet **Team Evaluation: Customer Service** in their handouts or workbooks.

SCRIPT: For your first assignment, you will complete this two-step team evaluation.

In Step 1, you are asked to put your heads together, and I'd like you to do just that. Discuss the four questions that follow. [*Read the questions aloud.*] Decide on the answers and then record them.

In Step 2, I've listed complaints that customers typically have about service people. Do any of these apply to us? Have you heard any customer complaints not listed here? When you have answered these questions, note each complaint that we need to work on. You don't need to write out the complaint, just note its list number. How frequently do you think the complaint occurs? Why you do think it occurs? What suggestions do you have to eliminate it? Obviously, some of the things you discussed in Step 1 will reappear here, and that's fine.

Does anyone have any questions about what I'm asking you to do? [*Answer questions.*] You have 30 minutes for this exercise. Go.

LEADER'S NOTE: Thirty minutes is the recommended time for this exercise, but you can modify it as needed. During the exercise, roam around the room to ensure teams are on track and questions are answered. At the end of the designated time, call the teams to attention and begin the feedback process.

3. Solicit Feedback, Set Priorities, Create Action Plans   50–60 min.

LEADER'S NOTE: Because of their interactive nature, the first two parts of this subsection are unscripted. Your task is to do the following:

- Be present and keep an open mind.

- Listen attentively to what team members discover about themselves.

- Ask questions for clarification.

- Affirm members' perceptions when appropriate.

- Add your own assessments backed by specific examples.

> **● Optional Discussion Topic:**
> **The Cash-Register Culture**
>
> If this issue is pertinent to your team, introduce the idea of the "cash-register culture" from Chapter 1 somewhere in this section. Define what it is and lead a discussion based on the following questions:
>
> - What is our cash-register culture?
> - Does it stop us from focusing in our customers?
> - What can we do keep our service focus?

- Guide the discussion from problems to solutions.

- Help the team identify two or three priorities that would have an immediate impact on their ability to deliver excellent service.

- Assure the team that other problems they've identified will be addressed in future meetings.

- Remind note-takers to submit key discussion points to you after the program, preferably in an electronic format.

LEADER'S NOTE: After debriefing the team, engage them in action planning on two or three top priorities (see our worksheet **Priorities for Implementation**). What actions will team members take to solve a problem or to eliminate a complaint? Who will be accountable for the activity? When will the solution be implemented? Who will be responsible for following up the implementation?

Remember: Action planning is a thinking skill, and one of your overall program goals is to teach front-liners how to think and create results not only today but also in the future. Begin by uncovering a few issues, training your team how to handle them, and creating simple processes they can apply as new issues arise. (When you have peer leaders in place, you'll be able to provide more extensive support to reinforce these skills.)

Either have the team work as a large group to create action plans for each priority, or break into small groups with each tackling a different item. For the latter, allow 15 to 20 minutes for groups to devise a plan, write it on a flip chart, and present it to the entire group.

Whatever your approach, solicit input from everyone to refine the plan and gain commitment. Also ensure everyone receives a copy of every action plan for future reference. This material can be stored in your customer service binder or a common computer file.

4. Facilitate Individual Evaluations   10–15 min.

LEADER'S NOTE: Our worksheet **Self-Evaluation: Customer Service** is designed for this section.

SCRIPT: Now that we've committed to important actions as a team, let's wrap up this evaluation section with one final topic: How well are *you* doing as a contributor to our customer service efforts? Take a look at the self-evaluation on [*page in participant materials*]. No one but you will see this today, so be honest with yourself. You and I will discuss your answers privately at our next one-on-one meeting in the coming week [*or other time frame*], so be sure to bring this page along.

Also, I'm looking for peer leaders to help me implement our customer service initiatives. If you're interested in the position and/or want to nominate someone else for it, please let me know in your answers to the evaluation's last two questions. At lunchtime [*or next break or other free time*], I will touch base with each of you to collect your recommendations. I want to start identifying, selecting, and training peer leaders right away. They will help us follow up on our commitments today and assist me in keeping the momentum going. Any questions? [*Entertain questions.*]

You have 10 minutes to complete this evaluation.

LEADER'S NOTE: Based on the size of your team, determine how many peer leaders you'll need. A practical ratio, for example, would be one for every seven front-liners. Remember: When recruiting, focus on high-level performers, those who receive nominations from a substantial number of their peers, and those who indicate a willingness to serve in that capacity.

SECTION A—REVIEW

SCRIPT: Before we move on to the second part of our program, let's do a quick review of what we've covered so far.

LEADER'S NOTE: Spend 5 minutes or so summarizing the high points of Section A. For example, repeat your "sales message." If it fits your style, engage your team in a "mini pep rally," shouting each key sentence of the message. Have fun with this and repeat it periodically throughout the program. These key sentences will become part of the "reminders" assignment you give them at the end of the day.

Review the priorities the team has committed to, re-inforce your expectations for continued participation, entertain questions, and tie up loose ends. Make this a summary statement as well as the bridge to the next section.

Section B: Strategies and Training

5. Teach Strategies for "Always Under-Promise and Over-Deliver"   45–60 min.

SCRIPT: I want to begin this training session with the most basic principle of customer service: Always under-promise and over-deliver. You've heard that dozens of times, and it's so important that you'll hear it dozens more. Our challenge is to discover how we can make this principle a practical, everyday part of how we do business with each and every customer. [*Direct members to location in handouts or workbook.*]

SCRIPT: What do we mean by "Always under-promise and over-deliver"? [*Take responses.*]

● *The Number 1 Principle:*
"Always under-promise and over-deliver."

- Meet expectations:
  — Make it right, make it easy, make it fast.
- Exceed expectations:
  — How right? More than the customer could have possibly expected.
  — How easy? Easier than the customer could have possibly expected.
  — How fast? Faster than the customer could have possibly expected.

Give me some examples of how you use this principle in dealing with customers every day. [*Take responses.*]

LEADER'S NOTE: Draw on your experience to lead a discussion of what the principle specifically means in your business. Here are some essential guidelines:

- Ensure that team members know the parameters of "under-promise" and "over-deliver" in terms of timing, costs, flexibility, customization, and any other criteria important to the delivery of your products and services. Don't take their understanding for granted. Be ready with everyday examples of how to implement this principle. For instance:

  —A bookstore tells a customer that the book he ordered will arrive in seven to 10 business days. They call five days later to say it's in.

—A car dealership gives a repair estimate based on the maximum charge for parts and labor. When the customer picks up her car, the bill is less than the estimate.

—Restaurant customers want to exchange salad for soup, fruit for fries, provolone for parmesan. How flexible can the server be?

—A piece of clothing is slightly soiled and the customer asks for a price reduction. How far can the salesperson go?

- Stress the following: "Don't get carried away lowering expectations. We don't want customers to walk away from our business. We have guidelines for when and how to promise customers a bit less than whatever we know we can deliver." Clearly explain your guidelines. If you have included them in your participant materials, refer members to them.

- Relate the principle to your business:

  —Meeting expectations means the interaction with the customer is "right, easy, and fast." What does that look, sound, and feel like in our business?

  —Exceeding expectations means making "right, easy, and fast" go farther than customers expect. How do we do this in our business? How can we do this?

- If appropriate, discuss the idea of "free stuff" (see Chapter 4.) Pose the following questions, take responses, and set guidelines.

—Once we've served a customer "extra right, extra easy, and extra fast," how can we still go above and beyond?

—What kind of "free stuff" can we offer to exceed customers' expectations? Discuss the possibility of samples and add-ons.

Conclude this section by taking questions. Tell team members that improving on the "under-promise, over-deliver" principle is an ongoing concern, and that you will welcome any future recommendations based on their day-to-day experience.

6. Facilitate Training in Communication Skills   45–60 min.

LEADER'S NOTE: Let your team know that today you will present an overview of fundamentals and that in the weeks ahead you will follow up with more in-depth lessons and specific practice.

If your business has preset communication guidelines, include them in this section; also, see our handout, **The Eight Keys to Successful Communication.** Again, customize your presentation based on your best practices as well as on our suggested basics.

SCRIPT: If we want to deliver great service, we have to be great communicators and great problem-solvers. Communication and problem solving are the two essential skills we will focus on—and practice—in this part of our program.

Both of these skills are highly valuable because you can use them in any area of your life—in your personal relationships as well as your professional ones. They're life skills as well as customer service skills, and can have a dramatic impact on your success beyond this program and beyond this business.

To begin, let's take a look at the eight keys to successful communication. [*Direct members to location in their participant materials.*]

The first key is "Make yourself available." Obviously, to respond to customer needs, we have to "be there." What does being "available" look like, sound like, feel like on this team? [*Elicit responses.*]

LEADER'S NOTE: Here is a chance to review and reinforce the guidelines you've already taught. Engage members in a discussion of what they do well and not so well when it comes to "availability." Return to script when you are ready to summarize the discussion.

SCRIPT: Being available means being present both physically and mentally. You must be visible to customers and attentive to their words and actions.

This leads us to the second key: "Listening carefully." Listening is the forgotten communication skill. We spend so much time talking—both out loud and in our heads—that our own chatter often drowns out what other people are saying. Yet listening is essential to building any relationship. Do any of you have friends who are great listeners? [*Take show of hands.*] Then you know what I mean. Listening is a sign of respect as well as caring.

When it comes to the skill of listening here at work, there are several basic tactics to remember.

The first is "Use both eyes and ears." Listen to a person's words and tone of voice; also watch the person's body language—facial expressions, hand gestures, and posture. Communication is a combination of words, tone, and body language, and a great listener learns to pay attention to all three.

LEADER'S NOTE: Illustrate the above with a real-life example of how you listened to a customer on all three levels –words, tone, body language—to determine what the customer needed or wanted. Engage team members in sharing their own examples.

SCRIPT: The next tactic is "Don't interrupt when someone is speaking." You want the customer to feel like the most important person in the world to you right now.

Of course, sometimes another customer interrupts the conversation. What do you do when that happens? [*Elicit responses. Either reinforce the preset guidelines for such a situation or use the following.*] In such a case, respectfully tell the interrupting customer you'll be with him or her momentarily; or, if you know your first customer will take time, refer the second to another service person. In either case, return to your first customer, apologize for the interruption, and give him or her your full attention.

This attention takes concentration. This is why our third tactic is "Don't let your mind wander: Concentrate." Really focus on the customer and his or her expressed wants or needs. Also, make sure you're clear on those wants or needs by asking the customer questions—our fourth tactic. Being a great listener also means being a great questioner. What kind of questions can you ask to get a better picture of what the customer wants or needs? [*Elicit responses. Refer to our suggestions in Chapter 4 and ask the team to record other appropriate questions.*]

Finally, ask specific questions to ensure you understand what the customer is saying—our fifth tactic. What kind of questions can you ask to confirm your understanding? [*Elicit responses. Again, refer to suggestions in Chapter 4 and ask your team to record other appropriate questions.*]

Our third communication key—"Say as little as possible"—is usually difficult, as most of us like to talk. But consider this: The less you say, the less chance there is to say something distracting, confusing, annoying, wrong, or offensive. The less you say, the more "air time" you give your customers. The less you say, the more time you have to choose your words carefully.

Of course, saying as little as possible doesn't mean saying nothing. It means you listen carefully, you stop and think, you choose the right words, and you respond appropriately.

How do you find the "right words"? We'll work on that by creating a variety of materials for finding those "right words" and the most professional information about our products and services. In fact, in the weeks ahead, we'll begin a process to get us all involved in creating what I call "just-in-time information tools." I want you to have the most thorough and precise explanations and responses at your fingertips. We'll talk more about that during another team meeting.

The next communication key—"Be truthful"—is a basic principle about which there are no arguments. You must *always* be truthful. This may seem like a no-brainer, but sometimes, in our enthusiasm to close a sale or give customers a quick answer, we slip off base. And "being truthful" goes far beyond never lying to customers. We must be aware of how small inaccuracies can damage the customer's trust. What do I mean? Beware of hopes, guesses, and exaggerations.

LEADER'S NOTE: Offer examples from your own experience and/or from your observations of team members. Don't embarrass any one individual, but do use situations they can all identify with.

SCRIPT: Of course, sometimes you don't know the answer to a customer's question. In that case, what should you say? [*Elicit responses.*]

LEADER'S NOTE: Guide members as they answer this question, leading them to "I don't know. Let me find out for you." If appropriate, make sure they include "Let me collect your contact information so I can get the correct answer to you when I find it." See if members have any questions of their own before moving on.

SCRIPT: The sixth communication key is "Request feedback." As you all know, we ask for customers' feedback in a variety of ways.

LEADER'S NOTE: Comment on the feedback processes already in place in your business. Then, focus on the next learning point for your team.

SCRIPT: The kind of feedback I want all of you to get from our customers is quite simple. You need to make sure that each and every customer is happy about their interactions with us and has no unsatisfied expectation or need at the moment. How are you going to do that? [*Elicit responses.*]

LEADER'S NOTE: Guide your team toward creating a series of questions they can use to achieve the desired result. These may include: "Is that acceptable?," "Are you happy with everything?," and "Is there anything else you need?"

SCRIPT: It's obvious by now that the words you choose to say—or not to say—have a tremendous impact on customer relationships. How you phrase a question and how you respond to a question can enhance or hurt any interaction. So it's appropriate that the last two keys to successful communication have to do with words: words I'd like you always to say and words I'd like you never to say.

LEADER'S NOTE: If your organization provides front-liners with its own script for various types of customer interactions, then draw on that script now and reinforce its importance. There are two options here:

- Offer your team a chance to rehearse. Be sure to have scripts available and set up role-plays with that end in mind. Of course, you'll need to extend the time frame of this section accordingly.

- Tell your team you'll review the scripts with them at a future team meeting because you want to focus on the basic rules of polite interaction.

SCRIPT: First, the "always say." This is not rocket science—I simply want you to follow the basic rules of politeness with every customer. When greeting a customer, what are you going to say? [*Elicit responses, moving them toward your preferred greeting.*] After an interaction with a customer, what are you going to say? [*Elicit responses, moving them toward your preferred closure.*]

Of course, throughout any conversation, when it's appropriate, say, "Please," "Thank you," and "You're welcome." I'll be listening carefully for these words during the coming week. So every time you see me, a gong should go off in your head: "[*Your name*] is listening. I'd better be polite!"

LEADER'S NOTE: Try not to be too heavy-handed here, but let the team know you are serious about wanting them to be polite. Then see if they have any questions before moving on.

SCRIPT: Finally, let's consider the "never say" list. What should you never say? [*Elicit responses.*]

LEADER'S NOTE: Be sure to consider the "never say" items on our list: cursing, negative comments about others, and "I can't help you." You may want to add others such as "We can't do that," "We won't do that," "This is company policy," "It's not my job," "I don't work in this department." Also, jargon that customers won't understand.

LEADER'S NOTE: These communication tips can become part of the "reminders" you'll challenge your team to create at the end of the day.

7. Facilitate Training in Problem-Solving Skills 75–90 min.

LEADER'S NOTE: For this topic, you can use our handout—**The Six Keys to Successful Problem-Solving**—or create one of your own.

SCRIPT: One of the most satisfying and challenging parts of any customer service job is being a problem-solver. When customers call us on the phone or walk in our door, they want the assurance that we can solve their problems and come up with solutions. They want the assurance that we are experts in our field and can deliver what they need or want, even when they don't know what that is.

Of course, problem solving can mean a variety of things. Is anyone willing to comment on how you're a problem-solver here at work? [*Elicit responses and cover the following points.*]

Problem solving could mean educating customers on products and services that they want to know about or that they don't even know exist. It could mean handling customer complaints quickly and courteously. It could mean dealing with out-of-control, in-your-face people who seem to blame you for every bad day they've had for the past decade. Have any of you ever had one of those? Since you lived to talk about it, would you like to share the experience? [*Say the latter light-heartedly and elicit responses. Feel free to share some of your own "war stories" about irate customers and how you did—or didn't—handle the situation well.*]

In the weeks ahead, we'll spend much more time on how to deal with those extreme cases, but today I want to focus on some basic guidelines you can use immediately to become more effective problem-solvers. As you'll see, several of the things that we've just learned about communication are specifically applicable here. Great problem-solvers are great communicators.

We had eight keys to successful communication. Now we have six keys to successful problem-solving. [*Direct members to location in participant materials.*]

The first key is "Be on the lookout for problems great and small." That means no ostriches allowed on this team. I want all of us to be awake and aware of things that are missing, out of place, or broken. I want you to watch for glitches, hassles, misinformation, and anything else that makes the customer's experience less than right, easy, and fast. And I definitely want you to pay very close attention to customers' complaints. For example, let's look at the following problems.

LEADER'S NOTE: Offer examples of recent "problems great and small" that your team has tackled or failed to tackle. You may want to announce a contest with prizes for those who spot and resolve significant customer service problems. Fun activities with incentives will definitely produce positive results throughout your intervention.

SCRIPT: Now let's look at our second key, "Distinguish between problems you can solve and those you can't solve." Obviously, the more experience you have, the more problems you will be able to solve. Those are the ones I want you to handle expediently and professionally. If you have the skill, ability, and authority to fix the problem, go for it. And if it's something that happens again, I want you to bring it to my attention immediately. I don't want you to keep investing your time and energy fighting fires if we can put out the blaze once and for all.

Does anyone have any recent experiences of tackling a problem, only to have it recur? [*Encourage discussion. Have someone record the recurring problems, and inform the team that these are areas you'll all address in the near future.*]

Of course, even the most seasoned employee can be stumped by a new situation or request and not be sure what to do about it. That's why we have the fourth problem-solving key, "Give special treatment to bigger problems"—gather information, pass it to the right person as soon as possible, and follow up on the problem.

LEADER'S NOTE: Make sure you know how and to whom the necessary information is passed in your organization. Your team must be clear on (1) the details they need in order to gather the information, and (2) the channels they can go through to get immediate answers and support. (In Stage 3 you'll find specific training sessions on standard operating procedures for handling complaints; for now, simply offer the basics.)

Stress that once the problem has been passed on, the front-liner is still responsible for follow-up until he or she receives confirmation that the problem has been solved and the customer is satisfied.

SCRIPT: Our fifth problem-solving key is "Engage complaining customers." Take a quick look at the list of tactics. What do you notice? [*Elicit responses.*] They're the same ones we just covered in our communication discussion. It's one thing to be available, listen carefully, or be truthful when people are being nice; it's another when they're angry, upset, or frustrated. And when they're in your face, it's certainly a challenge to remember what questions to ask and what to say and what not to say. That's why it's important to practice the communication skills every day: If they become part of your communication style, you'll find it easier to draw on them when you're under stress.

If you look at each of these tactics in the context of handling complaints, you'll see some slight variations. For example, make yourself available by asking questions such as "Is something wrong? What can I do to help you?" Our customers want the assurance that someone is going to help them on the spot; so if you ask these questions with caring and respect, you can lessen their frustration, anxiety, and anger right away.

Customers also want us to listen carefully. Of course, you're going to be attentive and not interrupt, especially if emotions are running high. But you do need to engage them with specific, clarifying questions such as "Do you mean—?" Or, "Do I understand correctly that you are saying—?" Of course, they want you to fix the problem or get them what they need and want— yesterday. But until you can figure out what that is, customers need to know you are on their side. Listening and asking great questions will convey that.

Again, say as little as possible, rely on our prepared materials, and be truthful.

Now when it comes to "Request feedback," there are several things I want you to keep in mind. Once you have a plan to solve the customer's problem or have received information from someone who can, share your plan with the customer, get their input, and ask if this approach is satisfactory. [*Offer an example of what doing that would sound like in your business.*]

Great questions are the key to success. What kinds of questions can you ask to move your customer toward a satisfactory resolution? [*Elicit responses and make the following suggestions.*] How about questions like, "What can we do to resolve this situation for you?" Sometimes customers have already formulated a plan that will satisfy them and that, ultimately, will cost us less time, energy, and money. [*Offer an example from your own experience in which a customer was less demanding than expected—one in which you would have offered more if you hadn't asked for the customer's input first.*]

If the customer has no suggestions, move on to "Here's what we can do to resolve this issue [*or* handle this situation]. How does that sound to you?" Whatever approach works with your customer, get his or her "OK" to proceed with the solution. Finally, remember that it's still your problem until the customer is satisfied, so you will have to follow up to ensure satisfaction.

On the "Always say" list is, of course, "I am sorry" and "Thank you for bringing this to my attention." As for the "Never say" list, never say things like "I can't help you" or "We can't do that." And never argue— you're here to serve customers, not to engage in a battle. They may be argumentative, but you don't need to be. [*Offer examples from your experience in which you "blew it" with a customer by arguing, or in which you kept calm in the face of their anger or frustration and solved the problem.*]

Is there anything you'd like to add to the "Always say" or "Never say" list that you've found helpful when in the problem-solving mode? [*Entertain responses.*]

LEADER'S NOTE: If you already have lists, reinforce them. If not, you may want to add: Always say ...

- "I agree. This is not up to our usual standard of excellent service."

- "I'm going to do everything I can to make this right."

- "What would you recommend as a satisfactory resolution to this situation?"

SCRIPT: Are there any other questions about problem-solving tactics? [*Answer questions.*] OK, now let's try these tactics on for size with some role-playing.

LEADER'S NOTE: Young service employees have told us they find role-playing a valuable learning tool. The chance to try out communication and problem-solving tactics before they "hit the floor" raises their comfort level and lessens their stress level. So don't under-estimate the power of these exercises. Make them fun. Be creative. Keep them brief and focused on the real-life situations your people encounter every day. In fact, before you begin the training program, ask some of your seasoned employees to help you write scripts. Engage them in playing the customer role and ask them to prepare "push backs" when appropriate to challenge your front-liners to think on their feet.

Part 3. Team Project and Wrap-Up

**8. Engage Team in
   Creating "Reminders"**   **35–45 min.**

LEADER'S NOTE: For this topic, see our worksheet **From Learning Points to Reminders**.

SCRIPT: [*Adopt a lighthearted tone.*] Does anyone remember everything we said today? Me, neither. That's why we all need constant reminders to keep us on track. If we're going to commit to customer service principles and tactics, we need to remember what they are. So I'd like to engage you in a four-step process to create a series of customer service reminders. I want you to be as creative as possible.

First of all, please turn to our worksheet. [*Direct them to its location in handouts or workbook.*] As you can see, I've summarized all the major learning points we've discussed today. Go down the list, topic by topic. Which learning points are the ones we need reminders for? Check them off.

Second, do we want to change the language in any way to customize it for our team, or do we want to leave the language as is? If you want to suggest changes, write the changes on your worksheet, below the learning points.

Third, what form will our reminders take? For example, would it be helpful to put the reminders on a sheet or business card by the phone or cash register so you can make quick reference to them? Would it be fun to have something like "Take care of our customers and we'll take care of you" on a personal mug? Do we want to use posters, signs, or T-shirts to publicize to our customers that we're committed to dazzling customer service and want their input on how well we're doing? Be as creative as you can with ideas about what our reminders will look like.

Finally, are there any other slogans, sayings, or symbols that would help us remember our customer service commitment? How can we "brand-name" ourselves as a team that strives to deliver dazzling service? Does our team need a name and/or logo? These are just a few things to think about in this part of your discussion.

Are there any questions? [*Entertain questions.*]

LEADER'S NOTE: Break the team into groups and ask them to select a facilitator, timekeeper, and note-taker.

Allot 20 to 25 minutes for discussion. Of course, if the groups are fully engaged and need more time, be flexible. While members don't have to reach consensus on all the reminders, it's important they identify some of them and you get volunteers to work on creating displays to keep the "buzz" going after the program.

LEADER'S NOTE: When time is up, facilitate a feedback session and come to consensus on reminders the team wants to display. Ask for volunteers to form a "Creative Reminders Committee" (feel free to name this group as you wish); then schedule a time when the group can meet to draw up a plan of action. Negotiate a deadline for submitting to you a proposal that includes language, graphics, time frames, and budgets.

9. Summarize Commitments and Wrap Up Program   15–20 min.

LEADER'S NOTE: The summary is unscripted because it depends upon what you and your team accomplished during the program. Here are tips for what to include:

1. Summarize what you have covered today, from assessments and action plans to principles, tactics, and reminders.

2. Prioritize assignments for the near future, set deadlines, and clarify accountabilities. Assignments should include:

   - Implement the action plans that were created during the assessment process.

- Practice the tactics identified for the "under-promise and over-deliver" principle, and be prepared to discuss the challenges and triumphs at the next team meeting.

- Practice the eight communication keys. At the next meeting, be ready to report back on what worked and what didn't work.

- Be aware of recurring customer service problems that need to be solved, and report them as they happen. (Remember: Stage 3 offers suggestions for how to involve your team in creating a standard operating procedure for this task.)

3. Inform your team that you will schedule one-on-one meetings to discuss self-evaluations and to create performance improvement plans. You will also begin interviewing potential peer leaders. Once they are selected, you will start training them so they can help with the ongoing implementation of this program.

4. Finally, make your closing remarks. Be sure they're personal and passionate, based on your experience of the program. Also:

- Thank team members for their participation.

- Reiterate your commitment to the customer service initiative.

- Assure the team that you will coach and support them every step of the way.

- Re-emphasize that you are counting on their 100 percent participation and commitment.

If it fits your style, you can return to the customer service principles and close with a mini pep rally. You say, "Customer service." They respond, "It's non-negotiable." You say, "Customer service." They respond, "It makes work more enjoyable." And so forth.

Ongoing Training for Stage 2

After this initial training program, your team will need time to digest and practice what they learned. The next series of team meetings should focus on:

- The implementation of action plans
- Reinforcement of the eight communication keys
- Creating the "reminders"
- Discussions of recurring customer complaints.

Then, when you're ready, launch Stage 3.

● See the following pages for our suggested Stage 2 participant materials.

Assessment 2A
Team Evaluation: Customer Service

STEP ONE: How Great Is Our Customer Service Right Now?

Directions: Put your heads together and discuss these questions:

- *What are we doing very well?*
- *Where do we have room to improve?*
- *What is our biggest obstacle to delivering great service?*
- *What can we do to improve customer service?*

Once you have agreed on the answers, record them below.

STEP TWO: Customer Complaints

Directions: Listed below are 12 of the most common customer complaints about service people. Do customers ever complain about our team in any of these areas? Circle your answer. Even an infrequent complaint should be marked "Yes."

Complaints About Service People	Yes/No
1. We are nowhere to be found.	Y / N
2. We are present but unavailable to serve customers.	Y / N
3. We are available but rude, rushed, or indifferent.	Y / N
4. We are engaged and polite, but unknowledgeable.	Y / N
5. We provide customers with misinformation or conflicting information.	Y / N
6. We are too slow.	Y / N
7. We make mistakes.	Y / N

➡

Assessment 2A concluded

8. We unnecessarily complicate transactions.	Y / N
9. We are unable to solve small problems.	Y / N
10. We are unable to deal effectively with customer complaints.	Y / N
11. We embarrass customers for not doing something correctly.	Y / N
12. We fail to meet, much less exceed, customer expectations.	Y / N

Other complaints customers have about our team:

Now record all "Yes" complaints below, using their list numbers. How often do you hear the complaint—hourly, daily, weekly? Why does this complaint occur? What can you suggest we do to eliminate it?

Complaint	Frequency	Reasons	Suggestions

HANDOUT 2A

— Priorities for Implementation —

Action	Accountability	Deadline	Follow-Up (who & when)

Assessment 2B
Self-Evaluation: Customer Service

Directions: Answer the questions below as honestly as possible to evaluate your personal contributions to customer service.

1. Refer to the customer complaints you discussed with the team. Do customers make any of these complaints about you? If so, what specifically is their complaint? How often have you heard it? Why do you think they complain?

2. What can you do personally to improve customer service?

3. What is the biggest obstacle preventing you from delivering great customer service?

4. Are you willing to make a commitment to our customer service mission for this team and be held 100 percent accountable for it?

5. Are you willing to be a customer service peer leader?

6. Whom among your coworkers would you nominate to be a peer leader on customer service for this team?

HANDOUT 2B

The Eight Keys to Successful Communication

1. Make yourself available.

2. Listen carefully:
   - Use both eyes and ears.
   - Do not interrupt.
   - Concentrate on customer.
   - Ask open-ended questions.
   - Ask clarifying questions.

3. Say as little as possible.

4. Whenever possible, rely on prepared materials.

5. Be truthful:
   - Don't express hopes, makes guesses, or exaggerate aloud.
   - If you don't know the answer, try: "I don't know. Let me find out." If appropriate to your company, add: "Let me collect your contact information so I can get the correct answer to you when I find it."

6. Request feedback.
   - *How we ask for feedback:*

7. Always say ...
   - "How may I help you?"
   - "Are you happy with everything?"
   - "Is there anything else you need?"
   - "Please," "Thank you," "You're welcome."
   - *Others:*

8. Never say ...
   - Curse words
   - Negative remarks about a customer, coworker, or vendor
   - "I can't help you."
   - *Others:*

The Six Keys to Successful Problem-Solving

1. Be on the lookout for problems great and small.

2. Distinguish between problems you can solve and those you can't solve.

3. Solve small problems here and now if possible.

4. Give special treatment to bigger problems:
   • Gather information.
   • Pass the information to right person as soon as possible.
   • Follow up on the problem.

5. Engage complaining customers:
   • Make yourself available. Ask, "Is something wrong? What can I do to help you?"
   • Listen carefully. Be sure you understand the customer: "Do you mean [*insert what you think customer means*]?" And "Do I understand correctly that you are saying [*insert what you think the customer is saying*]?"
   • Say as little as possible.
   • Rely on our prepared materials whenever possible.
   • Be truthful.
   • Request feedback.
   • Always say "I am sorry" and "Thank you for bringing this to my attention."
   • Never say "I can't help you." And never argue.

6. Take ownership of customer complaints:
   • Follow steps 1 through 4 above.
   • Document customer complaint and record the date, time, nature of problem, and customer's name and contact information. Include any action you took to resolve the problem, the outcome, and the follow-up required.

   — Remember: It's your problem until it's solved —

HANDOUT_2D

Worksheet:

From Learning Points to Reminders

Directions: Review the list of learning points below and ask:
- *Which learning points do we want to use?*
- *Do we need to change the words?*
- *What form will the reminders take?*

Check off the points for which we need reminders. Also, record any suggested word changes in the space below the learning point.

CUSTOMER SERVICE PRINCIPLES

❏ Customer service is non-negotiable.

❏ Customer service makes work more enjoyable.

❏ Customer service makes everybody's job easier.

❏ Customer service is one of the most valuable skills you can possibly master.

❏ Every customer is a potential contact worth impressing.

❏ Take care of our customers and we'll take care of you!

THE MOST IMPORTANT CUSTOMER SERVICE PRINCIPLE

❏ Always under-promise and over-deliver!

THE EIGHT KEYS TO SUCCESSFUL COMMUNICATION

❏ Be available.

❏ Listen carefully and ask great questions.

➡

HANDOUT 2D

❑ Say as little as possible.

❑ Rely on prepared materials whenever possible.

❑ Be truthful.

❑ Request feedback.

❑ Always say ...

❑ Never say ...

THE SIX KEYS TO SUCCESSFUL PROBLEM-SOLVING

❑ Be on the lookout for problems great and small.

❑ Distinguish between problems you can solve and those you can't.

❑ Solve small problems here and now if possible.

❑ Give special treatment to bigger problems—gather information, pass the information to the right person, and follow up.

❑ Engage complaining customers.

❑ Take ownership of customer complaints.

Are there any slogans/sayings/symbols that would "brand-name" our team as the best in customer service?

• Worksheet concluded

Develop Just-in-Time Information Tools

From FAQs to SOPs to one-pagers, just-in-time information tools are among the best supports you can offer front-line service personnel. If your organization already has developed them, your job is simple: Ensure they're up-to-date and that your team uses them consistently. If there are gaps, your job is to engage your team in creating their own. In either case, revising, creating, and using these tools is an essential part of your intervention.

Realistically, you and your team will probably spend several months developing the materials in this stage. Even with the help of peer leaders, there's no shortcut to creating excellent information tools. The payoff, however, is worth the time. You end up with knowledgeable, confident front-liners who know where to go for the information they need—just-in-time.

Training Options

You have several options for developing these tools:

- Present the tools in a series of 15- to 20-minute modules. Describe one tool in each, offer examples, discuss a step-by-step development process, and assign intensive "homework."

- Offer a series of 60- to 90-minute workshops during which your team engages in lots of hands-on work.
- Combine topics into several half-day programs.

Whatever approach you take, count on holding short follow-up sessions to address revisions, questions, and training on specific tools.

Preparation

Before your first session, review the just-in-time information tools we discussed in Chapter 5:

1. Answers to frequently asked questions (FAQs)
2. One-page customer handouts
3. Basic service and product facts
4. Written standard operating procedures (SOPs)
5. "Go-to" people list
6. Complaint process guidelines and forms

Also, review any preexisting materials in your company that are pertinent to your team. Organize them by category and prepare a packet with tab dividers that you can add to your team's customer service binder. As tools are revised or created, insert them behind the appropriate tab.

For materials too lengthy for a binder, devise another strategy to ensure that front-liners have easy access to what they need when they need it. For example, create a "road map" describing where and how to find specific information—in a database, file cabinet, catalogue, or one-pager near the cash register. Of course, if you are using computer technology, "binders and tabs" become common files accessible to everyone.

Remember, "just-in-time" means precisely that: quick, easy access to information as needed. Merely having information is insufficient; people need to know how to access it immediately and use it consistently.

If you decide to use our recommended handouts, be sure that you prepare them for distribution or add them to your workbook. If computers are available, deliver the handouts electronically.

Program Outline

Since handling complaining customers is one of the most stressful aspects of any customer service job, we recommend that you begin with standard operating procedures for addressing and tracking customer complaints. Next, focus on a "go-to" list and FAQs. Finally, prioritize the remaining tools. Throughout this chapter, we offer suggestions for developing each, but the order is up to you.

Below is an outline of suggested topics presented in a workshop format. Our time frame for each workshop —60 to 90 minutes—can be adapted to your needs and priorities. Plan time between sessions for shorter meetings (15 to 20 minutes) to check on assignments, make revisions, and ensure your people know how, when, and where to use the specific tools.

— PROGRAM OUTLINE —

Workshop A: Kick-Off Session	**60–90 min.**
A1. Introduce the program	5–8 min.
A2. Evaluate the company's current information tools	45–70 min.
A3. Assign homework and schedule follow-up session(s)	10–12 min.
Workshop B: Create an SOP for Problem Solving	**60–90 min.**
B1. Review the six keys to successful problem-solving	10–15 min.
B2. Create the SOP	45–70 min.
B3. Wrap up the workshop	5 min.
Workshop C: Create an SOP for Tracking Customer Complaints	**60–90 min.**
C1. Review previous workshop and present introduction	10–15 min.
C2. Create a complaint tracker and an action plan	45–70 min.
C3. Wrap up the workshop	5 min.
Workshop D: Create a "Go-To" List	**60–90 min.**
D1. Review tools	20–25 min.
D2. Introduce "go-to" list of key people	35–45 min.

D3. Wrap up the workshop	5 min.
Workshop E: Create FAQs	**60–90 min.**
E1. Introduce the process	5–10 min.
E2. Facilitate answering FAQs	45–70 min.
E3. Wrap up the workshop	5–10 min.
Workshop F: Create One-Page Information Sheets	**60–90 min.**
F1. Introduce the process	5 min.
F2. Facilitate creating one-page information sheets	45–70 min.
F3. Wrap up the workshop	5 min.
Workshop G: Create SOPs for All Positions	**60–90 min.**
G1. Introduce the process	5–10 min.
G2. Facilitate the SOP process	45–70 min.
G3. Wrap up the workshop	5 min.

The following leader's guide covers each workshop and includes notes and suggested scripting. To make the guide easier to use, handouts are grouped at the guide's conclusion. There are five handouts in all:

- Analyzing Our Current Information Tools
- Most Frequent Customer Issues
- Complaint Tracker
- Answering Customer FAQs
- One-Page Information Sheet

Leader's Guide

Workshop A. Kick-Off Session   **60–90 min.**

A1. Introduce the Program   **5–8 min.**

SCRIPT: Today we're going to begin the process of creating just-in-time information tools. What are they? Tools that provide us with the most accurate, up-to-date information about our products and services as well as the best answers to customer questions, problems, and complaints. If we're going to be perceived as knowledgeable professionals, we need access to the best information—just-in-time, all the time.

Over the course of the next [*time frame in weeks or months*], we'll hold a series of workshops to create a variety of practical tools, from frequently asked customer questions to standard operating procedures that cover the major tasks we're accountable for.

During each workshop, we'll examine one specific information tool, get as much work done on it as time allows, and then create a process to continue the work until we're satisfied we have the best tool for now. The sooner we have basic tools in place and get everyone up to speed using them, the sooner we'll exceed our customers' expectations—consistently.

Of course, this will be an ongoing process. As new issues or problems arise, we'll address them as quickly as possible so no one is left "hanging." I want to ensure you have what you need when you need it to deliver excellent service. So, is everyone on board with a 100 percent commitment and willingness to participate in this important project? [*Call for a show of hands.*]

Here's the plan for today. Since we don't want to reinvent the wheel, we're going to start with the information tools the company already has developed. Here are some that apply to us. [*Hand out appropriate materials.*] I'd like you to evaluate these materials based on how effective and up-to-date they are. If we can find easier, faster, better ways to use them, we'll do that. If we find they're obsolete, we'll get rid of them.

A2. Evaluate the Company's Current Information Tools   45–70 min.

LEADER'S NOTE: Break your team into small groups of three to six members. Ask each group to select a facilitator, a timekeeper, and a note-taker. Make it clear that note-takers are responsible for delivering written results to you not only after the program but also after any follow-up discussions. If possible, provide note-takers with desk- or laptops so they can easily record results and send them to you electronically.

Divide material among groups. Select only material of immediate value. Handle on your own the more complicated tools or those beyond the team's expertise. While you want members' suggestions, you don't want to engage them in exercises that lead to confusion or frustration.

Provide a single-sheet "tool analysis" handout that can be attached to each tool, and instruct teams to analyze each tool based on the handout's questions (see **Analyzing Our Current Information Tools** handout). If computers are available, deliver the handout electronically and have groups use one per analysis.

LEADER'S NOTE: To familiarize members with this process, give them time to assess one tool; then ask for feedback. It's imperative they understand the process well enough to do their "homework" after the workshop. Answer questions for clarification, create models of what you want—an honest evaluation of each tool's practicality—and engage the team in assessing as many tools as time allows. Quality is more important than quantity at this point.

A3. Assign Homework and Schedule Follow-Up Session(s)   10–12 min.

LEADER'S NOTE: Assign small-group and individual work on the next set of in-house materials, set deadlines, and ensure that note-takers accept accountability for submitting written results. Inform the team that you will collate their responses and report back to them at the next team meeting (or next appropriate time.) As an alternative, ask peer leaders to meet with the small groups to check on progress, gather completed assignments, and deliver them to you.

Repeat this process until you are satisfied that all pertinent in-house tools are examined and updated.

Finally, build in time during a team meeting to ensure that everyone knows how to access the tools and use them just-in-time.

Be on the lookout for opportunities to recognize and reward outstanding contributors at the end of this project and those that follow.

Workshop B.
Create an SOP for Problem Solving   *60–90 min.*

B1. Review the Six Keys to
**   Successful Problem Solving   10–15 min.**

LEADER'S NOTE: If you created the customer service workbook we recommended in Stage 2, ask your team to bring it to this workshop. If not, provide a separate handout to review the previous problem-solving training (see Stage 2).

SCRIPT: The first new just-in-time information tool we're going to create is a standard operating procedure for handling customer problems and complaints. Before we tackle it, let's review the six keys to successful problem-solving that we discussed during our training program on [*date*].

Does anyone remember any of the keys? [*Facilitate a quick review. Be sure the team covers all six points.*]

OK. First of all, we need to create a standard operating procedure for how to handle customer problems or complaints that are within your discretion. We want to define (a) the parameters of that discretion, and (b) what to do when you don't know what to do. [*Ask lightheartedly.*] Does that make sense?

B2. Create the SOP   45–70 min.

LEADER'S NOTE: Divide your team into small groups of three to six members. Ask each group to select a facilitator, a timekeeper, and a note-taker. Ensure that note-takers accept accountability for submitting results to you after the workshop, preferably in an electronic format.

Ask groups to discuss the customer problems and complaints they encounter most frequently. Is there a policy that service personnel must follow? If not, do you need one? If one already exists, do service personnel have any flexibility with it? If not, what do they say to the customer? If they do have flexibility, what are the parameters?

Provide your team with the handout **Most Frequent Customer Issues.** Walk them through the process using an example from your business. Allow 20 to 25 minutes for discussion; then open the floor to feedback. Focus on the common issues raised among the groups and discuss each in terms of what to do, what to say, and what flexibility they have.

Since "Sorry, this is our policy" is one of the most dreaded statements customers hear, determine how front-liners should diplomatically state that a policy is, indeed, non-negotiable. Create a script that they can use in this situation.

Handle as many issues as you can within your time frame, and advise the team that you—or a peer leader—will organize and distribute the results in the form of an initial SOP. You will continue the discussion at subsequent meetings, so final revisions can be made. Once finalized, this SOP will become just that: a standard operating procedure. As new issues arise and are addressed, they can easily be added to this section of the customer service binder or computer file.

B3. Wrap Up the Workshop   5 min.

LEADER'S NOTE: Ask your team to look for other customer issues during the coming week that fall within the context of this SOP. Tell them to bring those issues to the next workshop, when you will engage them in creating an SOP for tracking customer complaints. Since these topics are closely related, consider scheduling the next workshop as soon as possible.

Workshop C.
Create an SOP for Tracking Complaints 60–90 min.

C1. Review Previous Workshop and
Present Introduction   10–15 min.

LEADER'S NOTE: Spend a few moments reviewing the last session. Check on any new situations that need to be added to the "Customer Issue" list, and clarify policies, flexibility, and parameters.

SCRIPT: The last time we met, we covered customer problems that are within your discretion to address. Today, we want to create a standard operating procedure to document two other types of customer complaints: (1) those that keep recurring—these are "fires" we need to put out once and for all—and (2) those that exceed your present knowledge and expertise. What do you do with those?

We're going to create a written documentation process to cover those bases and make it our next SOP. Why do we need written documentation?

LEADER'S NOTE: Open the floor to discussion. Be sure to cover the reasons for such documentation:

1. Written documentation protects front-liners as well as the organization if a customer says no action was taken.

2. It helps managers understand problems and complaints more clearly.

3. It identifies recurring "fires" that need immediate attention.

4. It becomes a training tool for how to handle similar situations in the future.

C2. Create a Complaint Tracker and an Action Plan   45–70 min.

LEADER'S NOTE: Customize the form in handout **Complaint Tracker** to fit your situation, distribute your version to the team, and discuss how to use it.

Entertain suggestions for revisions and then develop a step-by-step action plan to implement it. The tracker and action plan become your next SOP.

Open the floor to discussion on when the complaint tracker should be used. For example:

- When a problem or complaint repeatedly occurs (this is a "fire" that managers need to know about so they can address it once and for all)
- When a service person doesn't have the expertise or authority to handle a customer problem
- When the issue can't be resolved immediately and requires further investigation

Generate a list of everyday situations that would require a tracker.

Continue discussion by clarifying your "back-up strategy" for when a problem is beyond your front-liners' expertise but can be immediately addressed by someone else. What words should they say? For example:

- "That's a great question. Let me find someone who can give you a great answer."
- "I'm not 100 percent certain how to deal with this. Let me [find/contact] someone who can give you help immediately."

Also discuss guidelines for submitting the form:

- How soon after the event must it be completed?
- To whom should it be sent?

- How soon afterward should front-liners follow up with the recipient as well as with the customer?

Reinforce the principle "It's my problem until it's solved."

Conclude discussion by covering any other guidelines or parameters required by your situation.

C3. Wrap up the Workshop   5 min.

LEADER'S NOTE: Inform your team that you will distribute the revised tracker and action plan by whatever deadline you've chosen. Once they receive this material, it becomes another standard operating procedure for which they are accountable. You want them to test it out and be ready to report back on its "pros" and "cons" at the next team meeting or workshop.

Workshop D.
Create a "Go-To" List   *60–90 min.*

LEADER'S NOTE: Since your people need to know who has the information, experience, or expertise to handle particular products, services, or customer issues, the "go-to" list may be the next most practical tool to address.

D1. Review Tools   20–25 min.

LEADER'S NOTE: You and/or your peer leaders will do the initial homework for this workshop, so this session may be shorter than the others. If so, use the extra time to review and reinforce the work that the team accomplished during the last session. For example, check on how well the complaint tracker is working.

- Are there any glitches that need revision?
- Are there any new issues that need to be addressed?
- What challenges and triumphs have team members had in using it?

Open the floor to "stories" of their experiences.

D2. Introduce "Go-To" List of Key People   35–45 min.

LEADER'S NOTE: Prepare a list of products, services, and problem areas and a corresponding list of key people your front-liners can contact for information or support. Include other employees, managers, product/ service suppliers, consultants, and service providers, and give their contact information. Ideally, you want a minimum of two resource people for each area.

Discuss this list with team members and get their input on other areas where they may need help. Add those to the list with corresponding contacts.

Point out that the "go-to" list is another tool that will be amended as new issues arise and people change positions, gain expertise, or come into or leave the organization. Therefore, you want them to look for additions/corrections and submit those to you or a designated peer leader.

Finally, decide how to make this initial list easily accessible to everyone. Possibilities include putting it in a computer database, in their customer service binder, and on a sheet near phones or cash registers.

D3. Wrap Up the Workshop   5 min.

LEADER'S GUIDE: Summarize what you accomplished in this workshop; then give your team a preview of the next workshop. Let them know they will develop answers to customers' frequently asked questions, and assign them to pay close attention over the coming week(s) to the questions that customers consistently ask. They should record the questions and submit them to you, preferably electronically, by the deadline you specify.

Optional: Make this assignment a contest, and offer prizes for the quantity as well as quality of the FAQs.

Workshop E.
Create FAQs   *60–90 min.*

E1. Introduce the Process   5–10 min.

LEADER'S NOTE: Prepare a handout of the most common and pertinent customer questions your team submitted. By all means, add your own. Keep in mind that soon you'll have the team create one-page information sheets; therefore, put aside any questions that would be better addressed in that format, namely, those that require extensive details, specs, and specialized language.

Optional: Award prizes to those who contributed the most questions and the best questions.

SCRIPT: In our discussion of communication skills on [*date*], we learned that saying as little as possible is one of the keys to successful communication. However, that doesn't mean saying nothing. It means we listen carefully to what customers say, and choose the right words to respond appropriately.

What are the "right words"? That's the focus of today's workshop. First, we'll create rough drafts of the best answers to the questions you submitted; then we'll practice and refine them before we roll them out to our customers. It's one thing to have answers written down on paper; it's another to be able to deliver them clearly and confidently.

E2. Facilitate Answering FAQs   45–70 min.

LEADER'S NOTE: Break team into groups of three to six members, with a facilitator, a timekeeper, and a note-taker. Ask note-takers to submit final drafts to you after the program.

Facilitate the following five-step process:

1. Distribute a different set of five or six FAQs to each group. The FAQs should vary in complexity, with each printed on a large index card or a copy of the **Answering Customer FAQs** worksheet. Ask groups to brainstorm the answers, and instruct note-takers to write final versions on the cards or

sheets. Explain that the answers should be short and sweet. Offer examples from your own experience to serve as models. Print the examples on a handout, slide, transparency, or flip chart, so groups can see them throughout their discussion.

Considering the number and complexity of the questions, set a time frame (e.g., 20 to 25 minutes) for writing first drafts.

2. When time is up, ask group members to divide into dyads or triads, "fire" questions at one another, and take turns responding with the "scripted" answers. You want them to hear their written words spoken aloud. Ask them evaluate each response: How well does the response flow? Does it say what we really want it to say? Does it use the best words? Does it convey accurate information? Can we say it with fewer but more powerful words?

3. Have members return to their small groups. Instruct note-takers to make revisions based on this exercise and to record them under "Revision" on their cards or worksheets.

4. Explain that each group should now link up with another to trade questions and revisions. Challenge the partnered groups to improve each other's answers. Since they worked on different questions, they'll bring another perspective to the answers. Ask note-takers to add the critiques to their cards or worksheets.

5. Open the floor to a sampling of questions and answers and discuss which are the most effective. At this point, the quality of the examples is more important than the quantity. Since creating answers to FAQs is an ongoing project, you want to ensure that members can distinguish between excellent and mediocre responses.

Also, while it's your responsibility to review and finalize all answers, you want teach your front-liners how to write the best rough drafts possible.

E3. Wrap Up the Workshop   5–10 min.

LEADER'S NOTE: Collect the note-takers' work or ask them to send it to you electronically. Ask for volunteers to continue to work on this project, and divide the remaining questions among them. Set a deadline for submitting answers (preferably in an electronic format) to you or peer leaders.

Optional: Offer prizes for the quantity and quality of the answers.

Inform the team that you will review and edit their answers for distribution at the next team meeting (or next appropriate time). Let them know where the final FAQs will be stored (for instance, in the team's customer service binder or easily accessible database) and that additions will be made as the need arises.

Finally, create a process for practicing the finalized answers after the workshop. Here are some possibilities:

- Set up role-plays at the next team meeting.

- Have the team create an FAQ game with prizes. For example, print questions on business-card-sized stock and have members pull a card and answer the question. The person who answers the most questions accurately within a certain time frame wins.

- Ask peer leaders to quiz front-liners throughout the week, posing a question and asking for answers on the spot. Leaders keep a scorecard and the person who has the most accurate answers receives a prize. Of course, ensure that all front-liners are given equal opportunity to participate.

Workshop F.
Create One-Page Information Sheets   60–90 min.

LEADER'S NOTE: This workshop is an adjunct to the previous one. At this point in Stage 3, you may want to vary your approach by asking for volunteers to work on this tool or by inviting only members who have a talent for writing or graphic design to participate. You also may want to use a trained peer leader to head discussion and collate materials for your final approval. If none of these tips work for you, proceed with the entire team as usual.

F1. Introduce the Process   5 min.

SCRIPT: Now that we're really rolling with our FAQs, there is a complementary tool I'd like us to discuss: the one-page information sheet. What I'm thinking about is a graphically appealing, thoroughly accurate and detailed document about the services, products, processes, and issues that prompt lots of customer questions. In that way, when a customer asks a very detailed question that requires an even more detailed answer, we don't have to rely on our memories—we can hand over a great-looking one-pager with all the information the customer could possibly want.

What do you think that would feel like? You could give them a first-rate answer without uttering one word. Now that's powerful!

LEADER'S NOTE: If your business already has samples of one-page information tools, by all means, distribute models and discuss elements applicable to your team.

F2. Facilitate Creating One-Page Information Sheets   45–70 min.

LEADER'S NOTE: Involve the team in brainstorming a list of products, services, procedures, and issues that require a one-pager. Record the list on a flip chart and prioritize the items for development. Then divide the team into groups of two to three members and assign one priority to each group.

Offer a worksheet for creating a rough draft (see our handout **One-Page Information Sheet**), and set accountabilities for each document. Note that the groups will be responsible for creating content as well as graphics and layout.

Ask groups to discuss the information needed for their one-pager and the resources available to obtain it—people, catalogues, computer files, and so on. You want to teach them an effective process so they can continue to create these documents after the workshop.

Debrief room at large to ensure everyone is on the right track and understands the results you want.

F3. Wrap Up the Workshop   5 min.

LEADER'S NOTE: Divide the other priorities among groups, and ask them to commit to a series of deadlines to deliver completed one-pagers to you or a peer leader. For example, they may commit to completing one or two per week during the next month. You might ask your peer leader to collect them and to add his or her own suggestions before passing them on to you electronically. As with every information tool, you have the final say.

Schedule training time to address these tools during subsequent team meetings.

Finally, offer special recognition/rewards for people who work on this project.

Workshop G.
Create SOPs for All Positions   60–90 min.

LEADER'S NOTE: This workshop requires everyone's participation because SOPs should be prepared for every front-line task and responsibility.

G1. Introduce the Process   5-10 min.

SCRIPT: Today we will begin creating a series of standard operating procedures for our everyday tasks and accountabilities. We've already created two very important ones on handling customer problems and tracking complaints. Anyone remember what we did to develop them? [*Open the floor to discussion, and lead members toward next point.*]

SOPs are the most effective steps people can take to get results. In essence, each explains, "In this situation, to get this result, we do step one, step two, and so forth." In this way, if someone new joined the team, we could hand the new member our SOPs and get him or her up to speed much more quickly than ever before. So, the challenge is to make the SOPs easy to read and understand.

G2. Facilitate the SOP Process   45–70 min.

LEADER'S NOTE: Tell the team to form small groups of three to four members based on the similarity of their jobs (individuals with the most similar jobs thus form a group). Give them time to do this; then ask them to select a facilitator, a timekeeper, and a note-taker.

When ready, facilitate the five-step process below. Allow 20 to 25 minutes for the first three steps.

1. Ask groups to brainstorm a list of all the tasks and responsibilities with which they are charged and have direct experience. Record the list on a flip

chart. Keep groups on this step until the list is comprehensive.

2. Groups should now prioritize the tasks. Be sure to define your criteria (e.g., importance, frequency) before launching work on this step.

3. Instruct groups to draft a bullet-point SOP for their top priority on the flip chart. Stress that you are looking for clear, concise, step-by-step explanations for what they do and how they do it in order to achieve the best results.

4. Return to the room at large to debrief. Ask groups to take turns presenting their SOPs, and invite other members to make suggestions for improvement. At this point, you want to create models the entire team can use for ongoing development.

5. If your time frame allows, engage groups in working on their next priority. Debrief again and check for understanding. Gain commitment from groups that they will work on SOPs during the following weeks or months. Set deadlines and ask note-takers to electronically submit SOPS to you or a peer leader as the SOPs are completed.

G3. Wrap Up the Workshop   5 min.

LEADER'S NOTE: Again your job is to review the SOPs and finalize them. Let your team know that you will distribute each SOP as it is completed and expect the team to implement it. In short, from that point on, you will consider it indeed a standard operating procedure.

Creating Processes for Ongoing Development

Creating and updating just-in-time information tools is an ongoing process. For help, engage peer leaders in overseeing the next phases of this project. Specifically, ask each to head up the development of one or two categories. For example, one leader may be in charge of FAQs and one-pagers, while another may focus on SOPs for handling problems and complaints.

Once you have assigned accountabilities, be sure to do the following:

- Help peer leaders create procedures for how they will gather, share, revise and publish materials.

- Let front-liners know who's accountable for what information tool, and encourage them to funnel their ideas, issues, questions, and suggestions to the appropriate person.

- As part of the ongoing learning process that will be defined in Stage 4, have your peer leaders lead 15-minute updates and training on new tools as they are developed.

- Create a recognition and reward system for peer leaders and front-liners who consistently contribute to this customer service initiative.

● *See the following pages for our suggested Stage 3 participant materials.*

HANDOUT 3A

Worksheet:
Analyzing Our Current Information Tools

Directions: Record the name of the tool on which you are focusing; then answer the questions below to determine the tool's status.

Name of information document:

Analysis Questions

1. How "just-in-time" is this information tool?

2. How often do we use it?

3. How easy is it to use?

4. Does it need to be revised? If so, how?

5. How can we use it more effectively to enhance our customer service?

6. Is this tool worth having at all?

7. Can we create something better, faster, smarter?

Result (check one):

❑ Use as is

❑ Needs revision (see suggestions above)

❑ Can be used more effectively if ... (see above)

❑ Discard

HANDOUT 3B

Worksheet:
Most Frequent Customer Issues

Directions: List the most frequent customer problems and complaints that are within your realm of authority to address. For each one, ask:

- *Do we have a policy that covers this issue? If not, do we need one?*
- *What flexibility do we have to bend existing policy?*
- *What are the parameters for that flexibility (dollar amounts, warranties, quantity, time, etc.)?*

Issue	Policy	Flexibility	Parameters

We need a policy for the following situations:

When we have no discretion to bend a policy, this is what we say:

HANDOUT 3C

Complaint Tracker

Date: Time:

Customer Information

Name:

Account/Invoice Number:

Address:

Phone: Fax: E-mail:

Nature of Complaint/Problem:

How It Was Handled:

Outcome:

Follow-Up:

Signed: Date:

Submitted to: Date:

— Remember: It's my problem until it's solved —

HANDOUT 3D

Worksheet:

Answering Customer FAQs

Group members:

FAQ:

First-round response:

Revision:

Critique:

Final version:

One-Page Information Sheet

Product, Service, Procedure, Issue:

Information: Resources:

Accountabilities

Content:
Team member(s)   Deadline for final draft

Graphics and Layout:
Team member(s)   Deadline for final draft

Final copy will be sent to _____ by _____
                              (Manager/Peer Leader)   (Date)

Commit to Ongoing Service Training

Before introducing your team to new skills in customer service, we suggest that you review and reinforce the basics you presented in Stage 2. Use the Stage 2 worksheet "From Learning Points to Reminders" to design a series of review lessons for routine team meetings. For example, how well has your team translated the principle "Always under-promise and over-deliver" into everyday behaviors? How effectively are they using the eight communication keys and the six problem-solving keys?

Once your team is well on its way to mastering these skills, move on to Stage 4's "lessons of the week." Here you'll find five quarter-hour courses for your team meetings. Each 15- to 20-minute module includes:

- Training instructions
- Slides that you can use in a PowerPoint or transparency format
- A one-page handout

You can easily turn these lessons into contests and reward the front-liners who best implement them. You can print the slides and post them in the employee lunch room as reminders. You can train peer leaders to teach some of the lessons. Above all, you can be as creative as possible to make them fun, fast, and memorable.

Quarter-Hour Course Agenda

Adapt this seven-step agenda to review lessons as well as present new ones. When reviewing, use the Stage 2 handouts. When presenting new lessons, see our Stage 4 material. And don't forget—15 to 20 minutes is a short amount of time, so you'll need to move each course along at a fast pace.

— QUARTER-HOUR COURSE AGENDA —

1. Review the principles driving your team's customer service mission. Begin each lesson with a lively review of your "sales message." For example: "Customer service is non-negotiable," "It makes work more enjoyable," and so forth.

2. Introduce the lesson.

3. Explain and discuss the skill(s) to practice.

4. Conduct a team activity. Get the team involved in a case study, role-play, or brief brainstorming session.

5. Set goals for the week.

6. Assign accountability for follow-up.

7. Announce contest and prizes (if applicable).

Follow-Up Meeting Agenda

Determine which weekly lessons need follow-up sessions. During these, you are primarily the coach and facilitator. Base your approach on your observations during the week and the results of team assignments.

Be sure to check on how well members practiced the lesson: What did they do very well? Where do they still need to improve? What "unexpecteds" did they encounter that should be addressed? What coaching can you offer during this session? What awards can be distributed at this point? What follow-up learning needs to take place?

Based on the results, make assignments for the coming week. When the team is ready to move on, introduce the next training topic.

Other Preliminaries

Pacing Your Lessons—and Roles

Since mastering any new skill requires practice, present a new lesson one week and review and reinforce it the next—and maybe the next and the next. To do this, you must play three roles: that of the instructor who introduces fast, hard-hitting content; that of the coach who observes team members during the week, gives them on-the-spot feedback, and guides practice sessions during team meetings; and that of the facilitator who focuses team members on what they've learned and uncovers the strengths that lie within each of them. Of course, all three roles will overlap and each is essential to your intervention strategies.

Conceivably, the following five lessons could cover 10 to 15 weeks of training. It's your call. Your job is to balance "buzz" and "burnout"—to keep your team members engaged and excited about learning without sending them into overdrive. Ask your peer leaders to help you take the team's pulse, and make adjustments accordingly.

Multimedia Options

Before you roll out new lessons, assemble an in-house video crew to film brief interviews with people who are already performing well in these skill areas. Many young workers have a facility with video technology and would love to tackle this creative project. Engage some as interviewers and provide them with an initial list of questions.

Next, start creating your proprietary video training library by asking your crew to edit and catalogue the video clips according to topic. Along the way, add to the library by engaging your team in acting out customer service "dos and don'ts." Rather than spending training dollars on videos that may or may not fit your situation, you've customized your own—and given your team a great learning experience in the process.

Program Outline: The Five Quarter-Hour Courses

In each of these sessions, you are the instructor, delivering hard-hitting content and making weekly assignments. Allow approximately 15 minutes to present the lesson and 5 minutes to make the assignment and wrap up.

> ● *Why This Series?*
>
> When we asked young service employees what they most wanted to learn, hands down they responded, "How to handle angry customers." They did not mean just complaining customers, or those with problems to be solved, but customers who are overtly irate, even hostile. So that is why the Stage 4 courses deal with this issue.

— PROGRAM OUTLINE —

- Handling Irate Customers 101: Staying Calm in a Perfect Storm
- Handling Irate Customers 102: Laser Listening— What Are They Really Saying?
- Handling Irate Customers 103: Avoiding "Foot in Mouth" Disease
- Handling Irate Customers 104: Moving From Anger to Action
- Handling Irate Customers 105: Saying No Without Getting Punched Out

The following leader's guide provides you with the materials you need to present these training modules. Note that the slides and handouts are presented at the guide's conclusion, with one handout per module. As always, feel free to customize the material to fit your team's needs and your training style. Remember, in this setting, you are the instructor who drives the content.

Leader's Guide

Handling Irate Customers 101:
Staying Calm in a Perfect Storm

1. Review the Principles Driving Your Team's Customer Service Mission

2. Introduce the Lesson

SCRIPT: We've been working on problem-solving skills for a while now, so today I want to begin a five-part series on one of the most difficult problems in customer service: dealing with irate customers. You know who I mean—those angry, in-your-face customers who have already lost their cool and seem to be blaming every problem they've had since childhood on you and the business. [*Ask rhetorically.*] Ever meet one of those?

I'm calling today's lesson "Handling irate customers 101: Staying calm in a perfect storm." This handout will help you to follow along. [*Distribute copies of* **Handout 4A**.]

Here's the reality. When you're facing angry customers, you're dealing with two problems: first, the customers' emotions, and second, the problem that made them angry in the first place. Put the two together and there you are, caught in the middle of their perfect storm. At that moment, you have three choices ...

LEADER'S NOTE: Show **Slide 101.1**.

SCRIPT: You can remain indifferent—which will only enrage customers even more. Or, you can let them upset you—and if you're dealing with bullies, they have you where they want you. Or, you can use each contact to learn calming skills—which just might get the results the customer wants while also keeping you in good mental and physical health. Now which one do you think I suggest you choose? [*This is, of course, a rhetorical question.*] Right! Number three it is!

3. Explain and Discuss the Skill(s) to Practice.

SCRIPT: What are calming skills? There are four I'd like to share with you today and challenge you to practice during the coming week.

LEADER'S NOTE: Show **Slide 101.2**.

SCRIPT: The first is perhaps the most important of all and requires you to draw on your own emotional maturity. It simply says, "Keep your cool." Easier said than done, right? But this is a key to handling all the irate people in your life, not just here at work. One way to do that is by not taking the situation personally, even when you feel personally attacked. [*Offer an example from your own experience about what this looks, sounds, and feels like.*]

To help you separate yourself from the attacker, I want you to keep two things in mind. First, this fact: "I am a professional who is paid to treat people professionally. I will learn something from each encounter." No matter how unprofessionally customers are acting, no matter how rude they may be, you don't want to mirror their behavior. You need to hold your professional ground.

Second, I want you to focus on the customer problem or issue—not on the angry person in front of you. If you can ask yourself, "How can we solve this problem?," rather than focus on all the other nasty things that may be running through your head about the customer, then you're in a position of strength and you're in charge. You're not getting sucked into their emotions.

LEADER'S NOTE: Show **Slide 101.3**.

SCRIPT: To gain time to think, let the customer blow off steam. Often that's all irate people need: someone to listen as they vent. So you become the "ventilator."

You don't have to say anything at first. Just hold your ground, make eye contact without "staring out" the customer, stand firmly on your two feet for balance—or if you're sitting, put both feet firmly on the floor—breathe, and listen. It's important you be aware of your body. If you're swaying from side to side, or leaning heavily on one foot, or hyperventilating, you appear to be a "pushover." And you want to maintain that center of strength through your body language.

LEADER'S NOTE: Illustrate the above with your own body language. Be sure to include "comfortable eye contact." For this, make eye contact, hold it for a comfortable length of time (15 to 20 seconds), look away for a few seconds, then return. Teach the team the importance of making the connection but not staring out the person or looking everywhere but at the person.

SCRIPT: Whatever the situation, don't argue. Let me say that again: "Don't argue." Repeat it after me: "Don't argue." There's no need for a counter-attack. There's no need to defend our products or services. There's no need to rationalize anything. Irate people are too emotional to hear that kind of information anyway.

When it's clearly your turn to speak, immediately acknowledge the customer's anger. No big song and dance, just something brief and to the point, such as, "I'm sorry you feel this way. I can only imagine how angry and frustrated you must be." Don't say, "I know how you feel," because what can they shoot back at you? [*Elicit responses, leading to "No, you don't know how I feel!"*] Customers can't argue with you if you say, "I can only imagine." And you can say that sincerely.

Obviously, we don't want people angry with us, but the more professionally we can address the emotional part of the storm, the more easily we'll get to the other part: the real problem.

So, what are the four calming skills? [*Do a quick Q&A review.*]

4. Conduct a Team Activity

LEADER'S NOTE: If you have a video clip of an employee's encounter with an angry customer, use it—debrief what worked well and what didn't. If not, create a brief role-play of an angry customer "storming" at a front-liner (you might play the customer's part).

Instruct the front-liner to focus on calming skills and respond with the acknowledgment statement. Coach him or her on body posture, eye contact, and the tone of the statement. Ask: How does it feel to be yelled at? How did it feel to focus on the calming skills? Were you aware of your body during this encounter?

5. Set Goals for the Week

LEADER'S NOTE: Tell the team that you are going to post the slides (designate the places where you'll do this) and want them to look for opportunities to practice calming skills during the coming week. Obviously, members can practice the skills with irate customers. They can also pair up to create their own scripts of situations they've experienced or observed.

Instruct members to report back at the next meeting with either one or both of the following:

- Feedback on a real customer encounter. What happened? How did they use calming skills? What were the results?

- Two brief skits that illustrate "the dos and don'ts" of using calming skills. They should be prepared to act out their scripts.

On your part, consider videotaping the skits and adding the videos to your training library.

6. Assign Accountability for Follow-Up

LEADER'S NOTE: Everyone on the team is account-able for this assignment.

7. Announce Contest and Prizes

LEADER'S NOTE: If you wish, decide on a contest and prizes for this topic. You could offer small but meaningful prizes for the short-term result of the best story and/or script. A "small prize" might be an entry into a drawing for a larger prize down the line. Also, you might recognize and reward "The Irate Customer Handler(s)" of the month, the quarter, and the year.

Handling Irate Customers 102: Laser Listening—What Are They Really Saying?

1. Review the Principles Driving Your Team's Customer Service Mission

2. Introduce the Lesson

SCRIPT: At our last meeting, we focused one of the biggest challenges you face when confronted by irate customers: keeping your cool. Today we're moving on to the next challenge: making sure that we're clear on the real problem or issue so we can address it quickly and effectively. To do that, we're going to sharpen our listening skills. [*Distribute copies of Handout 4B.*]

3. Explain and Discuss the Skill(s) to Practice

SCRIPT: There are two related listening tactics I want you to be aware of and start to practice this week. These will make you a great listener in every area of your life, not just here at work, and are particularly important to practice when emotions are running high. Basically, they're the "laser surgery" that cuts through the anger the customer is throwing at you, so you can get to the real problems underneath.

LEADER'S NOTE: Show **Slide 102.1**.

SCRIPT: Those tactics are (1) check for understanding, and (2) repeat or paraphrase the complaint to acknowledge you heard it correctly. These tactics may sound simple, but they're not easy to put into practice. Let's take a closer look.

First, check for understanding. Picture an irate customer who is either spewing lots of words or saying practically nothing. In either case, you have no idea what the real problem is. It's hidden in the fog of the customer's emotions.

Of course, you keep your cool and acknowledge their feelings—and how are you going to do that? [*Elicit responses based on the previous lesson.*] Then, you prepare to check for understanding.

LEADER'S NOTE: Show **Slide 102.2**.

SCRIPT: There are several strategies for drawing more information out of the customer. For example, you can simply say, "Tell me more about ..." and fill in the blank with the appropriate words. [*Offer examples from your own experience; for instance, "Tell me more about why this product isn't serving your needs."*]

Or, you can say, "I want to make sure I've got this right. Would you repeat what happened one more time?" Another possibility is, "Help me to understand the situation so we can get this resolved quickly. Would you run that by me one more time?"

Does anyone have any other strategies that work for you? [*Open the floor to other suggestions and ask the team to add them to the handout.*]

Once you've checked for understanding, move on to the next tactic: Repeat or paraphrase the complaint to acknowledge you heard it correctly. You want to assure customers that you heard them clearly and have really got it right. This will calm them down and position you as someone who's there to help, not hassle.

Our lead-in statements are simple. You might say, "Let me make sure I heard you correctly"; or "Let me make sure I understand the problem correctly"; or "Let me see if I have all the facts here." Then comes the hard part: "What you're saying is ..." Depending on your ability at laser listening, what follows makes or breaks the conversation. Did you really nail it? Did you really understand the problem or the situation? And, there's no doubt about it, most customers will give you immediate feedback to let you know how well you did.

4. Conduct a Team Activity

LEADER'S NOTE: Create several role-plays based on situations in your business that might conclude with these statements:

- "This store [or business] always messes up!"
- "That's not what I was told the last time I called [or was in here]."
- "If I don't get better service, I'm going to call the Better Business Bureau!"

Ask one member to play the irate customer, and call on others to respond using the tactics you just presented. Make this interchange fun and fast-paced.

5. Set Goals for the Week

LEADER'S NOTE: Ask members to look for as many opportunities as possible to practice these tactics with customers and one another during the coming week.

Distribute scorecards–large index cards will do—and a strip of fun stickers. Ask the team to "stick it to" members who are caught handling an irate customer well or who respond effectively to instant practice sessions. Challenge them to do on-the-spot role-plays throughout the week based on their own experiences or on scenarios you and your peer leaders create and distribute randomly. Finally, ask them to bring their scorecards and examples of what did and what didn't work to the next meeting.

6. Assign Accountability for Follow-Up

LEADER'S NOTE: Everyone on the team is accountable for this assignment.

7. Announce Contest and Prizes

LEADER'S NOTE: The person who has the most stickers by the next team meeting receives a prize or is entered into a drawing.

Handling Irate Customers 103: Avoiding "Foot in Mouth" Disease

1. Review the Principles Driving Your Team's Customer Service Mission

2. Introduce the Lesson

SCRIPT: The last time we met, we focused on laser-listening tactics to better understand the customer's real problem. How can we figure out a solution if we're caught in the fog of a customer's anger and can't define the problem? We can't. That's why this week I want to talk about how to avoid creating more emotional fog by keeping your foot out of your mouth. [*Distribute copies of **Handout 4C**.*] Let's look at our handout.

3. Explain and Discuss the Skill(s) to Practice

SCRIPT: In our initial training on communication and problems solving, we worked with a list of things we should never say to customers. Do you remember? [*Elicit affirmative responses.*] Today I want to focus on what not to say especially when dealing with an irate customer.

LEADER'S NOTE: Show **Slide 103**. Read each line, asking after each, "If you say this, what would an irate customer say in return?" For example, the line "You should've told me that in the first place" will in- sult the customer and may provoke the response "I did say that, but you weren't listening." Keep this in- teraction fast-paced, upbeat, and fun.

4. Conduct a Team Activity

LEADER'S NOTE: Return to the "never say" list and ask members to recommend alternatives. You can either engage the entire team in this or break into groups for a 5-minute brainstorming session. Also, ask a peer leader to collect the best statements, to collate and distribute them right after the meeting, and to post them with today's slide.

5. Set Goals for the Week

LEADER'S NOTE: Challenge members to practice the best statements with customers and with one another throughout the week. (See scorecard method in lesson 102 as an option for recording successes.) Also, ask them to electronically submit other effective statements to you or a designated peer leader during the coming week.

6. Assign Accountability for Follow-Up

LEADER'S NOTE: Peer leaders are accountable for collating, distributing, and posting the best statements. Front-liners are accountable for practicing and submitting new alternatives. Print the best new responses (and best scorecards if using them) for the next meeting.

7. Announce Contest and Prizes

LEADER'S NOTE: You can use the best new responses (and best scorecards if applicable) as the basis for awarding prizes at the next meeting or entering winners in a drawing.

Handling Irate Customers 104: Moving From Anger to Action

1. Review the Principles Driving Your Team's Customer Service Mission

2. Introduce the Lesson

SCRIPT: So far, we've tackled calming skills, laser-listening skills, and "never say" statements. Today, I want to focus on action skills. How do we quickly and professionally assure customers that we're here to do something about their problem or complaint?

LEADER'S NOTE: Distribute copies of **Handout 4D** and show **Slide 104**.

3. Explain and Discuss the Skill(s) to Practice

SCRIPT: There are four steps we need to take to move from anger to action. [*Read steps from the slide.*] Let's look at each one individually and discuss some simple tactics to help us implement them.

First, "Explain the action you will personally take to correct the situation." At this point, you may know exactly what to do because the problem is within your realm of discretion to handle; or you may know exactly where to find the information you need, or whom to contact; or we may have a policy or standard operating procedure to cover the problem. [*Offer practical examples that would fit the latter scenario.*]

Whatever the case, it's important that the angry customer see you as someone who can—and will—do something to solve the problem. That assurance becomes part of the calming process.

Our second step is "Thank customers for bringing their concern to your attention." No big song or dance is needed here. A simple "Thank you for bringing this to my attention" will do. The trick is to say it as if you really mean it. [*Adopt lighthearted tone.*] And you do mean it because you are a professional problem-solver who just loves to handle people like them.

LEADER'S NOTE: If you have another approach, feel free to use it. But remember the bottom line: Saying less is more at this point in the interaction.

SCRIPT: We discussed the third step—"Follow through and follow up"—during initial training, when we created our standard operating procedure for problem-solving. You know it's your problem until it's solved, and if you've been practicing this step all along, it should be second-nature—even in the face of an irate person.

LEADER'S NOTE: In Stage 3, we recommended creating an SOP for handling complaints and a "go to" list of resources. If you haven't created these yet, make them a priority.

Use the fourth step from the slide if it's applicable to your business. And if it isn't, you might want to ask, "Why isn't it?"

SCRIPT: Finally, the fourth step is our goodwill gesture, our exceeding-customers'-expectation gesture: "Give them a freebie." For example ... [*Offer options that members can use in these situations. Ask them to recommend other things that you might add to your "freebie" list. Be sure to explain which free offer is appropriate for a variety of situations.*]

4. Conduct a Team Activity

LEADER'S NOTE: Create three or four role-plays that engage the team in using the tactics you just taught. Give them a synopsis of real-life scenarios they may encounter and that conclude with the customer asking, "And what are you going to do about it?"

5. Set Goals for the Week

LEADER'S NOTE: Challenge members to practice these tactics with customers and each other during the week. Ask peer leaders to spring "pop quizzes" on difficult situations. For example:

- "An irate customer returns an item, saying it's broken. However, it's not really broken—the customer just didn't follow the directions carefully. What are you going to do about it?"

- "An angry customer complains that the service we offered did not meet their expectations. What are you going to do about it?"

6. Assign Accountability for Follow-Up

LEADER'S NOTE: Peer leaders are accountable for giving pop quizzes, keeping score of great responses, and electronically submitting those responses to you before the next team meeting.

On your part, print the best new responses for use at the next meeting.

7. Announce Contest and Prizes

LEADER'S NOTE: Use the best responses to award prizes at your next meeting or to enter winners into a drawing.

Handling Irate Customers 105: Saying No Without Getting Punched Out

1. Review the Principles Driving Your Team's Customer Service Mission

2. Introduce the Lesson

SCRIPT: Let's face it: Sometimes we just can't give customers what they want and so we haven't any choice but to say no. However, if we say this bluntly, we may trigger even more anger in the already irate customer. Today you'll learn how to deal with such a situation by developing "option skills." These skills can be used whenever we have to say no politely and professionally, but they are particularly important to use with irate customers.

LEADER'S NOTE: Distribute copies of **Handout 4E** and show **Slide 105.1**.

3. Explain and Discuss the Skill(s) to Practice

SCRIPT: What are option skills? They are problem-solving tactics based on two things:

- First, a thorough knowledge of the alternatives. What can we offer when we can't give customers what they want? And I really mean "can't" because we're bound by necessary policies, regulations, and restrictions. [*Provide the team with some examples from your business.*]

- Second, these tactics are based on positioning statements that help us say no professionally by communicating that we're really offering assistance, not resistance.

Today we'll focus on the alternatives and the positioning statements that you know already exist in the business. [*Show **Slide 105.2**.*] These are additions to our "always say" lists from past training.

LEADER'S NOTE: You may want to discuss alternatives during the next team meeting if it becomes obvious your team has knowledge gaps. That discussion may result in another information tool.

For this lesson, do a sentence-completion exercise with the "always say" list, focusing on one statement at a time. Offer an example of an alternative to a product, service, policy, regulation, and so on. Then ask your team to add others. Advance to the next statement and repeat the process.

Here are two examples:

- "We don't want to make promises we can't deliver. Here's what we can do: We can have that item delivered to your home by 6:00 p.m. on Friday."

- "We don't want to make promises we can't deliver. Here's what we can do: I'll contact my manager to find out what leverage I have to reduce the price and give you a volume discount."

SCRIPT: These positioning statements involve more than saying the right words—you must also be aware of your tone of voice, your eye contact, and your body language. Does your tone, eyes, and body say, "I can't wait to get rid of you?" Or do they project a sincere interest in resolving the situation? The words are important, but equally important is how you deliver them. Do customers hear and see "Go away"? Or do they hear and see "Yes, I can help you"? Let's practice that right now.

4. Conduct a Team Activity

LEADER'S NOTE: Using your business as the background, create three or four scenarios in which irate customers can't find what they want or don't like what you have in stock. If available, use video clips that would fit this theme. Have the team practice responses, paying particular attention to their tone of voice, eye contact, and body language. Coach them on projecting the "Yes, I can help you" attitude.

5. Set Goals for the Week

LEADER'S NOTE: Tell members to find as many opportunities this week as possible to practice positioning statements with customers and one another. Ask peer leaders to role-play scenarios with each team member and, if video equipment is available, to tape the role-plays. Videotape will allow members to check their tone of voice, eye contact, and body language.

6. Assign Accountability for Follow-Up

LEADER'S NOTE: All members are accountable for practicing. Ask them to be prepared to report their experiences at the next meeting. In addition to this (or optionally), select video clips of individual training sessions as examples of "dos and don'ts."

7. Announce Contest and Prizes

LEADER'S GUIDE: Determine whether a contest is applicable for this session.

Announce the Final Exam

After you have presented and reinforced the five-part "Handling Irate Customers" series, announce a "final exam." Depending on the team's size and the testing format you choose, the exam may fill one or more team meetings. Here are some possibilities:

- Give a written test with questions such as:
  - What are the four calming skills? Give examples of how you've used them this past month.
  - How do you acknowledge a customer's anger?
  - Give examples of how to say no professionally. How have you used those examples during the past month?
  - What are some of the "never says," particularly when you're dealing with an angry customer? What are some alternatives?

- Give an oral exam in which you ask members to respond to questions like those above in front of their peers.

- Engage each member in a role-play in front of the entire team.

  — Ask peer leaders to prepare scripts and play irate customers with various complaints.

  — Set up the scenarios in such a way that each member has an opportunity to practice several of the tactics they learned.

  — Examples of scenarios:

    "A customer has just walked in, angry with a purchase he made. You're the first one to approach him. What do you do? What do you say?"

    "Imagine you have already acknowledged the feelings of an irate customer who was given misinformation about a product or service. What do you do next? What do you say?"

  — Allow 5 to 6 minutes per team member, videotape them, offer coaching on the spot, and use videos for follow-up coaching sessions.

Whatever method you choose, make final-exam time fun, upbeat, and meaningful. Also use it as an opportunity for recognition, rewards, and celebration.

● See the following pages for our suggested
Stage 4 participant materials.

HANDOUT 4A

Handling Irate Customers 101:
Staying Calm in a Perfect Storm

1. Keep your cool:

   - Don't take it personally.

   - Think: *I am a professional who is paid to treat people professionally. I will learn something from each encounter.*

   - Focus on the issue: *How can we solve this problem?*

2. Let the customer blow off steam.

3. Don't argue.

4. Acknowledge anger: *"I'm sorry you feel this way. I can only imagine how angry and frustrated you must be."*

ASSIGNMENT OF THE WEEK

Complete one or both of these assignments:

1. Watch for opportunities to practice calming skills with angry customers. Be prepared to report on the situation:

   - What happened?

   - How did you use calming skills?

   - What were the results?

   - What did you learn from the experience?

   - What could you do better next time?

2. Pair up with another team member and create two skits to illustrate the "dos and don'ts" of using calming skills effectively. Be prepared to present the skits at the next team meeting.

Handling Irate Customers 102:
Laser Listening—What Are They Really Saying?

Laser Listening: Two Basic Tactics

1. Check for understanding.

   • Strategies:

     — *"Tell me more about ..."*

     — *"I want to make sure I've got this right. Would you repeat what happened one more time?"*

     — *"Help me to understand the situation so we can get this resolved quickly. Would you run that by me one more time?"*

     — Other strategies:

2. Repeat or paraphrase the complaint to acknowledge that you heard it correctly.

   • Lead-ins:

     — *"Let me make sure I heard you correctly."*

     — *"I want to make sure I understand the problem correctly."*

     — *"Let me see if I have all the facts about the situation."*

   • Then:

     — *"What you're saying is ..."*

ASSIGNMENT OF THE WEEK

Practice and stick it to 'em!

HANDOUT 4C

Handling Irate Customers 103:
Avoiding "Foot in Mouth" Disease

Never say:

- *"You should have told me that in the first place."*
- *"You'll have to ..."*
- *"You must be mistaken."*
- *"Our salespeople messed up again."*
- *"This is the third time I've heard that complaint today."*
- *"I've never heard of that happening before."*
- *"It's that darned computer again."*
- *"There is nothing I can do about it."*
- *"I don't know."* [Period]

Alternatives:

ASSIGNMENT OF THE WEEK

Practice and stick it to 'em!

Handling Irate Customers 104: Moving From Anger to Action

Moving to Action: The Four Basic Steps

1. Explain the action you will personally take to correct the situation.

2. Thank the customers for bringing their concern to your attention.

3. Follow through and follow up.

4. Give the customer a freebie.

Free items:

Situations:

ASSIGNMENT OF THE WEEK

Practice these steps with customers and one another during the week. Be prepared for a pop quiz at any time.

Handling Irate Customers 105: Saying No Without Getting Punched Out

Option Skills

1. Alternatives

   • What are the alternatives?

   • How do we position them?

   Remember: Assist. Don't resist.

2. Positioning Statements

   Always say:

   • *"We don't want to make promises we can't deliver. Here's what we can do: ..."*

   • *"Here is a possibility ..."*

   • *"You can ..."*

   • *"We do have ..."*

   • *"I'll check into this right now, and get back to before ..."*

   • *"There is an alternative: ..."*

   • *"What options have you already considered that I may be able to assist you with?"*

ASSIGNMENT OF THE WEEK

Practice the positioning statements with customers and one another this week. Be aware of your tone of voice, eye contact, and body language. Tape a role-playing session with your peer leader.

Your choices ...

- **Be indifferent**
- **Let the customer upset you**
- **Use each contact to learn calming skills**

● The Four Calming Skills

Skill 1. Keep your cool …

- Don't take the situation personally.

- Think: *I am a professional who is paid to treat people professionally. I will learn something from each encounter.*

- Focus on the issue: *How can we solve this problem?*

- The Four Calming Skills

  Skill 2. Let the customer blow
  off steam.

  Skill 3. Don't argue.

  Skill 4. Acknowledge the
  customer's anger.

● Laser Listening: Two Basic Tactics

1. Check for understanding.

2. Repeat or paraphrase the complaint to acknowledge that you heard it correctly.

1. Check for Understanding: Strategies

- *"Tell me more about ..."*

- *"I want to make sure I've got this right. Would you repeat what happened one more time?"*

- *"Help me to understand the situation so we can get this resolved quickly. Would you run that by me one more time?"*

2. Repeat or Paraphrase Complaint: Lead-ins

- "Let me make sure I heard you correctly."

- "Let me make sure I understand the problem correctly."

- "Let me see if I have all the facts about the situation."

☞ **"What you're saying is ..."**

Never say ...

- "You should have told me that in the first place."
- "You'll have to ..."
- "You must be mistaken."
- "Our salespeople messed up again."
- "This is the third time I've heard that complaint today."
- "I've never heard of that happening before."
- "It's that darned computer again."
- "There is nothing I can do about it."
- "I don't know." [Period]

- **Moving to Action:**
  The Four Basic Steps

  1. Explain the action you will personally take to correct the situation.

  2. Thank customers for bringing their concern to your attention.

  3. Follow through and follow up.

  4. Give the customer a freebie.

● Option Skills

1. What are the alternatives?

2. How do we position them?

☞ *Remember: Assist. Don't resist.*

Always say ...

- *"We don't want to make promises we can't deliver. Here's what we can do: ..."*
- *"Here is a possibility: ..."*
- *"You can ..."*
- *"We do have ..."*
- *"I'll check into this right now and get back to you before ..."*
- *"There is an alternative: ..."*
- *"What options have you already considered that I may be able to assist you with?"*